PROCESS EXCELLENCE FOR IT OPERATIONS

A Practical Guide for IT Service Process Management

MR PRAFULL VERMA and
MR KALYAN KUMAR B

ISBN: 0615877524
ISBN 13: 9780615877525
Revised Feb 2014

Trademark Acknowledgement:

ITIL is the registered trademark of Office of Government Commerce
CobiT is the registered trademark of the Information Systems Audit and Control Association
(ISACA)
CMM and CMMI are the registered trademarks of Carnegie Mellon University

In addition, many of the designations used by product vendors and other organizations
to distinguish their products and services and may be claimed as the trademarks or
service marks. Authors acknowledge such designations and used those designations in
initial caps or all caps.

ACKNOWLEDGEMENTS

Author Acknowledgements

I would like to express my thanks to the many people who supported and helped me to bring out this book; to all those who provided support, talked things over, read, wrote, offered comments and remarks and assisted in the editing.

While many of my colleagues and friends offered comments to refine the content, the origin of this inspiration is all my work in Cross Functional Services in IT Operations and for that, I would like to thank C Vijayakumar (Head of Global Infrastructure Services Delivery at HCL Technologies) for his utmost belief in the concept of Cross Functional Services (CFS) as a separate and critical service discipline in the area of IT services. He not only gave me an opportunity to work in this area, but also helped in bringing together various silos into one integrated team to realize the full potential of process excellence in IT operations through the Cross Functional Services. He also provided relentless support and guidance to realize the full vision of CFS over the last several years. I would also like to thank the entire CFS team who really inspired us to pen these thoughts into a book. The CFS team's quest for excellence and belief in the vision of CFS is the fuel for this and many more publications to come.

I would like to mention special thanks for my close friend Kavindra Sharma who talked over with me on the subject from Application Management perspective and offered valuable remarks to make the book interesting for larger set of audiences.

Last but not the least, I want to thank my wife, Annie who has been a constant source of motivation and encouragement for this project. I would not have started this without her active support. Annie stood by me and shared the excruciating work in helping me with typing and editing etc I also want to thank my daughter, Naomi who demonstrated a larger degree of patience during my work.

Finally I beg forgiveness of all those who have been with me over the course of the project and whose names I have failed to mention.

Prafull Verma

Co Author Acknowledgements

I would like to acknowledge the support of my Better Half, Zulfia who provided me the space and freedom to focus on this endeavor and also on my Musical Journey by carving out some family time. I would like to acknowledge the important teaching from my four year old kid Azlan who keeps teaching me that Child is the Father of Man"

Kalyan Kumar

"This book is dedicated to all the people who are busy in day to day IT operations. These are the soldiers of IT frontier and facing many challenges because of lack or poor Service Management strategy and yet win over the battle with their hard work"

TABLE OF CONTENTS

1 FOREWORD

Over the last 3 decades, the contribution of Services to Global GDP has increased exponentially. As per United States GDP data, the services contributed to 64% of the GDP in 1982 and this is close to 80% in 2012. The growth in services contribution to the GDP is even more remarkable in emerging economies, like the BRICS countries. This has been fuelled by exponentially increasing appetite for Service consumption, Innovations fuelled by technology adaption, higher levels of standardization and commoditization of services. IT has contributed immensely to the growth of services over the decades. Along with the growth of services, came the numerous conveniences in life that has enhanced the quality of life. IT Management is core to maintaining and enhancing the benefits that IT Services provide to individuals, businesses, governments and NGO.

Due to the growth as well as the criticality of IT Management, IT Services and the IT Outsourcing industry has flourished over the last three decades. The three key attributes that define IT Services are Service Definition, Service Measurement and Continuous Service Improvement. These 3 key attributes are very important for the success of any outsourcing relationship between the client and the service providers. The trend of growth and expansion in service industry will continue, hence the long term success of any service provider will depend on how effective and service oriented IT operations are in place.

All ITSM (IT Service Management) practices attempt to build on these attributes. There are several standards that has helped shape the IT Services space like ITIL, CMMI for Services, COBIT, ISO etc.,. While these standards bring in an excellent high level guidance towards IT operations, practitioners feel the need for practical guidance and specific ways of achieving Service excellence in IT Operations.

Prafull Verma, a colleague of mine at HCL Technologies, Infrastructure Services Division, has been highly regarded for his valuable insights in the IT Service Management, by Process consultants, Process operations specialists, Service Delivery Managers and Service designers at HCL. Prafull's interactions with the customers and industry experts has always resulted in a "WOW" and awe on the practical insights that he shares and their applicability in bringing excellence in IT Operations. This work of Prafull captures all the key aspects of how to bring in Service excellence in IT Operations. All IT Services practitioners in Service Provider space and IT professionals in the Client organizations will immensely benefit from this work.

The special Chapter on "Service Management for Cloud ...." has been authored by Kalyan Kumar (KK), another colleague at HCL, who is a visionary in adaption of new technologies and service practices far ahead of the industry and shaping them to bring in valuable benefits to businesses. With the increasing adaption of Cloud and "as a service" offerings, numerous Service Management challenges and complexities needs to be addressed to ensure Service Excellence. This chapter provides valuable insights towards this.

Although the book is primarily focusing on IT Operations but several principles are either applicable or already in practice in other service industries. The functional process model and the detailed process structure explained in this book can be used to design and analyze processes for non IT services also.

The good part of the book is that you do not need to be a technologist to read and appreciate the service excellence concepts and understand the ways of implementing them in your professions.

C Vijayakumar

Corporate Vice President and Global Head of Infrastructure Service Delivery, HCL Technologies Ltd.

2 INTRODUCTION

Process engineering is very commonly practiced in manufacturing industries, as processes are essential for all production. Process excellence in the manufacturing industry, revolutionized by the six-sigma approach, is an essential prerequisite to stay in the business. Business process reengineering has been a hot topic since the 1980s in the USA. This was the time when Japanese cars started entering the US market, and the might of Japanese manufacturing processes was revealed. One of the most talked-about processes was the "just in time" inventory management process that helped to reduce the manufacturing cost without compromising the quality. In those days, manufacturing was at its prime in the USA and we have witnesses the remarkable growth of manufacturing industry and its success attributed to the process excellence.

In the past three decades, economies all over the world have seen a tremendous growth in the service sector. The service industry also has followed the basic principles of process engineering to "produce" defect-free services. However, the application of those principles has not been very easy because of fundamental differences between product and services.

Process Excellence in Information Technology Operations

Beginning in 1990, the IT service industry emerged rapidly. IT customers are also becoming increasingly savvy in their use of IT and IT services. These customers are more demanding and have a better understanding of their IT needs. In order to address the service needs of savvy customers, you need to engineer savvy methods. In other words, you need to follow the footsteps of process excellence in the manufacturing industry to produce excellent services in the IT industry. Engineering as a discipline is very well used in all technology product-manufacturing areas but completely ignored in the IT service-management area. While providing a variety of guidance for process excellence, I intend to bring those engineering concepts that can bring the same outcome in IT service as realized in products and technology, so that the quality and reliability of service matches that of products. By using process-engineering concepts in the IT service area, people can create wonders.

Although a vast amount of material is available on IT service management, none addresses the need for guidance at a fundamental level.

There is ITIL (Information Technology Information Library), which helps to adopt a process-led approach and process framework established by OGC (office of government commerce, UK) to manage the IT infrastructure services in British government departments. ITIL provides a consistent and coherent set of processes that are deemed to be best practice, but that is still not a prescriptive process that you can take as is. It is top-level guidance but not a solution.

There is CMMI SVC, (Capability Maturity Model for Service) which is guidance on process improvement and focuses on process maturity but does not help to design the processes. CMMI® (Capability Maturity Model® Integration) models are collections of best practices that help organizations to improve their processes. These models are developed by product teams with members from industry, government, and the Carnegie Mellon® Software Engineering

Institute (SEI). This model, called CMMI for Services (CMMI-SVC), provides a comprehensive integrated set of guidelines for providing superior services.

We have COBIT, (Control Objectives for Information and Related Technology is a framework created by ISACA for information technology (IT) management and IT governance.) which provides exhaustive guidance for process controls primarily from a governance and risk-management perspective rather than from a service-management perspective.

Then there is an ISO/IEC20000 standard developed by International Standard Organization that promotes the adoption of an integrated process approach and certifies the processes that are being followed against its own standards.

All of above are kinds of service-management framework and building blocks for service-management architecture. But where is the process design and engineering guidance? And where is the process-management emphasis?

This is the vacuum that this book is attempting to fill in. The concept of process engineering as available and applied to business processes is altogether missing in this area. I am an engineer by profession and believe that IT service-management (ITSM) practitioners deserve some engineering guidance; hence I decided to fill in the vacuum. I also believe this book is the first of this kind of publication but will not remain the only one of this kind.

The book will be addressed to all IT people from a process-practitioner perspective; however, the fundamentals are presented in simplistic terms, and therefore it should be useful to all IT people. It will describe the process design and engineering concept as well as the process management concept and how it can be applied to IT service management. This is not about industry standard frameworks, such as ITIL and COBIT, but about the common processes that are generally used in real-life operations. I will be using analogies and illustrations from the non-IT world also to make things simple. This book will not focus on any technology.

The book will go beyond process engineering and illustrate how those engineered processes work and operate. For this purpose we will also add supporting topics.

Ubiquity of Process

During my work with different organizations, I have come across one very common statement made by IT managers: "We do not have any process." This is like saying that no one was breathing before Carl Wilhelm discovered the existence of oxygen in 1773. If people are doing something, and people are producing something (such as a service), it means there is some process to do these things. It is more appropriate to say that we have an ad hoc, undefined, ineffective, and inefficient process and/or multiple versions of a process for the same purpose, and each person may choose some part randomly to deliver. Or you may say that you design an ad hoc process in real time for that particular instance and to deliver the work. Work may go on without well-defined or official processes. If you do not define official processes, then they will be defined by default. Process by default will produce output, but it may not be the good quality you desire, the output may be expensive because of process inefficiency, or the output may be delayed and lose its relevance to business.

This situation raises the very fundamental need of having one official process and then adhering to it. An official process serves as a reference for everyone in the organization and guides toward a common goal, procedure, and policy. In the absence of a formal and official process, everyone follows their own version of informal goals, procedures, and policies. Therefore, inconsistencies are added in the system over a period of time. If you have one official process, even with defects, for the stated purpose, and it is not working, then you at least know which process needs to change or amend.

Technology Management is not good enough

The basic flaw in the IT service management world is that technology management is deemed to be service management, and thus the deployment of tools to manage the technology is deemed to be the process implementation. This flaw is even more expanded with clouds, as more and more tools are coming in to manage clouds.

Technology management is a part of service management, as it is the core part of producing the service; but it is not the service management. Does FedEx focus on cargo aircraft fleet management alone to manage their service? Airlines have strong standards on aircraft maintenance, but that maintenance does not count as service. A true service management will focus on managing the outcome, via how a customer (individual and organization) is realizing the benefit from the technology and will continue to realize benefit, so long as service is active or contracted.

The key areas that I intend to include are how to design, implement, and maintain processes for consistent IT operations.

Challenging the status quo

One of the driving factors to write this book was a strong urge to challenge the artificial stupidity that is prevailing in the IT service management (ITSM) world these days. People are all born ignorant, but they are not born stupid. Much of the stupidity in the IT industry in all aspects of technology—and more specifically in the area of process and tool implementation that we see today (tool implementation is deemed to be process implementation)—is induced by our IT research companies and industry analysts in collaboration with vendors. In a high-tech age that has seen the creation of artificial intelligence by computers, I also see the creation of artificial stupidity by people who call themselves research analysts/consultants but who promote the vested interests of product vendors by directing innovative propaganda or marketing gimmicks. Software products are promoted as the magic wand –out of the box solution to solve all business problems.

Research analysts and consultants are obligated to propagate the right knowledge, experience, and practices of the industry that went before them; research centers have instead been turned into selfish ideology centers to promote the vested interests of product vendors.

Many neutral IT professionals (and minority, like me) have protested against the specific things with which CIOs and IT managers are being indoctrinated. I am not sure if the hands-on experiences of IT professionals on the ground can help to overcome the relentless propaganda. For my own satisfaction, even if I think that IT professionals will overcome propaganda, I am afraid what may persist is the habit of hearing one side of story and making conclusions without hearing the other side—and, more fundamentally, without having developed any wisdom that would enable you to systematically test one set of beliefs against another.

The statement of many research companies that "our goal is to educate you how to make decisions, not what decision to make" can no more be taken at face value, because most of our research companies and research analysts today are teaching what decision to make—about everything from an end-user device to other hardware and software to service.

Many of today's "analysts" not only supply their customers with conclusions but also promote the idea that customers should make decisions based on these prepackaged conclusions — in other words, analysts vent their feelings and use propaganda with no authoritative knowledge of what is truth in those campaigns or the intellectual discipline to know how to analyze opposing arguments. Even if all the conclusions with which they indoctrinate were fully correct, that process would still not be equipping CIOs and IT managers with the wisdom to evaluate opposing views in order to be prepared for new and unpredictable issues that will arise.

I am also seeing the shadow of celebrity culture in the IT industry brought in by these propaganda. In the US, celebrities are created out of nothing. We have seen the phenomenal rise of celebrities. Celebrities do nothing without getting paid, and, even though some are talentless, they get stingingly rich just by being celebrities. Similarly, there are celebrity products created out of hype. Customers pay premium on these products because these are promoted as the renowned products in the industry.

There are varieties of symptoms that manifest an artificial stupidity, and one of the common themes is to invent some pleasing terminology and create propaganda around that. For example, I frequently come across two commonly misused terminologies—*transformation* and *value addition*. Transformation is a process of profound and radical change that orients the IT organization in a new direction and takes it to an entirely different level of effectiveness. Transformation is not "turnaround," which implies incremental progress on the same plane. Transformation implies a basic change of character and little or no resemblance with the past configuration or structure. In most IT organizations, *transformation* has become a very loosely used term applied to any project such as virtualization, new tool implementation, or bringing in some new products.

Similarly, *value addition* is another misused terminology. Before we talk about value addition, we need to debate on the meaning of *value*. The value denotes the worth of the service or desirability of the service, often linked to usefulness or utility. Value is a trade-off between benefits and costs and can be calculated as benefits divided by costs, where benefits are the financial and nonfinancial advantage to customers and are derived from the outcome of service, and costs are the financial and nonfinancial expenditure required of customers to receive the benefits.

While the costs of providing IT services may be well understood, the service benefits to IT customers are rarely understood. In fact, nonfinancial costs are also not understood very well. Although customers may appreciate the benefits from a service, they often cannot see what it costs them. If we apply the value equation from the customer perspective, we find that for customers to appreciate the value of IT services, they must be aware of costs. This means that the cost of the service must be known. Without cost awareness, customers would tend to maximize service value by maximizing service benefits through demanding higher service levels, either as increased service capacity or greater service-performance levels. Awareness of price forces customers to think about their service-level demands. They are compelled to perform the cost-benefit analysis themselves to determine the value to them, thereby adjusting the service consumption. (This is also one of the demand management principles.)

In most cases, customers seeking value additions are unilateral in applying formula; that is, they do not want to consider costs. Service providers attempt to demonstrate value additions by making some positive additions to service attributes. But any positive addition of any attribute of a service may not necessarily constitute value to the customer. At the end of this book, we will understand that "process" can be a key instrument in value addition.

Service Management Architecture

Yet another point I want to bring out is the need of service-management architecture. All organizations understand the need of architecture to deal with the growing complexity of rapidly expanding IT ecosystems. It helps to manage the costs as well, as it helps to elongate the ecosystem's lifespan of a system by finite future-proofing. A well designed architecture will help to maintain the usability of the system for a longer duration of time. While there is a well-known recognition of the need for architecture in a variety of technology areas, such as network architecture, application architecture, and data architecture, there is rarely any focus on service management architecture. How the lack of architecture makes the system unusable can be cited with a prominent example of Winchester Mystery House in San Jose, California.

In 1884, a wealthy widow named Sarah L. Winchester began a construction project of such magnitude that it was to occupy the lives of carpenters and craftsmen until her death thirty-eight years later. The Victorian mansion, designed and built by the Winchester rifle heiress, is filled with so many unexplained oddities that it has come to be known as the Winchester Mystery House. It took 38 years for 147 builders to construct the house, but there was no architectural plan. The house has 160 rooms, 40 bedrooms, 6 kitchens, 2 basements, 950 doors, 65 doors to blank walls, 13 staircases abandoned, and 24 skylights in floors. You will find staircases leading to nowhere and even doors in the floor. For this multimillion-dollar mansion (awfully expensive in that era), no architectural blueprint exists—Mrs. Winchester never had a master set of blueprints but did sketch out individual rooms on paper and even tablecloths!

While Sara Winchester defied the need for architectural planning, and we ridicule her ignorance today, we need to note that she was not running a business but pursuing her hobby. I am sure that we understand that we are in business—the IT service business—and are obligated to make a business proposition; therefore, we cannot afford to ignore service-management architecture.

2.1 Business-Focused IT Service

The universal problem today is that IT organizations are technology-focused. They think technology, and they build their living habits around technology. For the last several years, business-aligned IT (BAIT) has been a buzzword promoting the alignment of information technology with the business rather than with only technology. The real need is a step beyond that. In fact, business alignment is no more a differentiating factor and does not give any competitive edge. Every organization is deemed to be business-aligned. However, that does not mean that you can ignore business alignment, because if you do, you will be disadvantaged. Having BAIT is not an advantage, but not having BAIT is a disadvantage. I will emphasize business-*oriented* IT (BOIT) rather than business-*aligned* IT. BOIT will be possible only if IT becomes a business by itself. In other words, all the concepts of business management are replicated in IT management. When I say all the concepts of business management, those concepts are not limited to the finance, profit and loss, budgets, ROI (Return on Investment), ROCE(Return on capital Employed), and so on but the whole business management, and one important part of business today is business process management. Consequently, process management for IT services would become a cornerstone of business-oriented IT. BOIT will automatically be BAIT. In fact, BOIT is the next level—higher than BAIT—in IT value-chain status.

Successful businesses have been talking about process-driven organization that treats the business process as a portfolio of valuable corporate assets. Different businesses producing the same kind of products or services create brand names based on their processes. Perhaps the entire world knows the process for making a burger, but McDonald's burger-making process is the asset that is minting money for McDonald's. Today, all the airlines are using the aircraft produced by Boeing or Airbus. They are using the same airport runways and airport terminals. Yet there is a huge difference between the qualities of service among the airlines. (It is interesting to know that none of the airlines from North America or Europe figure among the top ten best airlines, according to www.airlinequality.com. It is also interesting to note that the airlines in North America have mechanized most of the services. They have ignored the human part of the service.)

The impact and significance of business processes are even more significant in the service industry. Service industries are investing a huge amount of money in business process management. Advance tools and techniques are used for business process management to define and execute processes in a manner that creates significant benefits. While the business process still runs on the IT and is enabled by IT applications, strong business-management techniques are making a fundamental shift by making the business processes more agile and yet liberated from IT applications. If we apply the corresponding analogy, a business-oriented IT or BOIT will be characterized by the following:

1. BOIT will be process-driven and will treat the ITSM process as a portfolio of valuable IT assets.

2. ITSM will be an overarching discipline across the entire IT sector, and significant investments will be made on managing the ITSM processes.

3. ITSM processes will be agile and liberated from technological tools.

There is yet another similar concept that is being propagated in the context of technology tools, and that is "ERP of IT." The basic idea is the same as BOIT; what is being done by SAP to an enterprise business should be adopted by IT organizations as well. This means each IT process will be owned and managed in the same way a business process is owned and managed.

3 UNDERSTANDING SERVICE ASPECTS

3.1 *Product vs. Service*

Service is an intangible set of benefits, created by a series of activities. Over the last decade in the IT industry, the distinction between "products" and "services" is blurred, as products are positioned as services, and services are packaged as products. To blur the distinction between products and services is more of a marketing strategy and does not constitute real differentiation. Not only will the sales and pricing strategy between products and services greatly differ, but so will the management approach.

Solution is not service, either.

IT infrastructure and applications are becoming increasingly packaged and commoditized. Adoptions of common industry standards have contributed to the commoditization of products. Mergers and acquisitions have resulted in the number of suppliers for technology products reduced to a handful of major vendors in many areas of the IT industry. Packaged solutions and SaaS have reduced the need for in-house, custom-built solutions. These developments have enabled a more "building block" approach to IT solutions, where many of the blocks can be bought whole, resulting in a level of commonality not previously possible. These packaged blocks are used to build solutions and presented as "service" to customers, especially in the area of the emerging cloud computing market. However, these solutions are not services.

3.2 Service Characteristics

Following are certain key characteristics that make services significantly different products.

Intangibility

Services—being benefits or activities—cannot be seen, felt, tasted, or touched, as products can. Consequently, services cannot be inventoried, services cannot be patented, services cannot be readily displayed or communicated, and pricing is more difficult. Please note that services can be performed by machines also; and, in fact, machines perform the major part of IT service activities.

Over the past several decades, the market share of the service-industry economy has grown significantly. This phenomenon has led to the development of several models and theories to tackle the intangibility problem. Now, in several service areas, we can get some sense of tangibility. The difficulty in pricing is also being overcome because of several cost models being adopted in the market. In a strong market economy, the price of the service is rarely based on what it costs but on how much the market can bear.

Process engineering also helps to address this problem. Well-defined processes allow estimating the cost of process execution. Also, process engineering increases the visibility of the result and its value.

Heterogeneity

Heterogeneity refers to a composition of dissimilar parts. Because services are created by activities, and activities are performed by humans (and automated/

assisted by machines), services tend to be more heterogeneous than products are. Consequently, service delivery and customer satisfaction depend on the provider's actions and the process that binds those actions together to make the service complete. Service quality depends on factors that are difficult to control; for example, the ability of the customer to articulate his or her needs, the ability and willingness of personnel to satisfy those needs, the presence or absence of other customers, and the level of demand for the service.

Heterogeneity is the primary cause of inconsistency of service quality, especially when actions are performed by people. In various kinds of services, the heterogeneity problem can be addressed by replacing human actions with machine actions. That is the key driver of all IT service automation, because it not only saves the cost and increases the speed of service but also eliminates the inconsistency. It is important to note that you need to automate sound logic and good process, else you will end up producing a consistently bad result (albeit faster and with less effort).

Design of robust processes will also help to address this problem.

Real-time nature

Services are produced and consumed simultaneously, whereas for products, production and consumption can be separated. The production of the service creates the "set of benefits," whose consumption cannot be postponed. Consequently, customers participate in and affect the transaction while consuming the service; a customer may impact the service level of another customer, the service provider's resources (or lack thereof) may impact the service outcome, and centralization and mass production are difficult. For example, if too many customers are simultaneously accessing some service, the performance may degrade, or if one customer is taking a longer time on the phone with a service desk agent, another customer may have to wait. We see in this in many other service areas also. If you are flying and the passenger in your next seat does not show up, your service level increases automatically.

This real-time nature is as if services were riding on an arrow of time, and elapsed time cannot be regained. "Productizing" of services has defied these constraints to some extent. In many cases, the products are presented as service, and this characteristic is completely defied; however, the service that requires real-time interaction will have inherent constraints for separating production and consumption.

Process design approach for real-time service production and consumption scenarios is different than that for non-real-time service production and consumption. For example, a service desk queue management process within an incident management process can address real-time service aspects.

Perishability

Services cannot be saved or stored. Consequently, it is difficult to synchronize supply and demand with services, and services cannot be returned or resold.

This characteristic is partially derived from services' real-time nature. Productizing certain services can partially tackle this constraint also. Some kinds of services may have an expiration period, after which their utility is lost, but productizing may provide some residual value. One example is mobile communication—you may store and use a voice message, but its utility might be lost after some time, and you may still have some value in old messages.

The difference between products and services may not be absolutely clear-cut all the time. Often, services are bundled or augmented with products to make them more tangible; for example, a monitoring service with security appliances. In the same way, products are augmented with add-on services; for example, a maintenance support contract/warranty to improve the quality perception of the buyer.

Design for optimized processes with resource optimization helps to eliminate the production of wasteful services.

3.2.1 Service Characteristics Illustrated

With a clear understanding of IT service delivery and IT service support, we can apply service characteristics to both of them. Since both are services, after all, both will have similar characteristics but will differ only in the degree of a particular characteristic.

Service Characteristic	Help-Desk Service	E-Mail Service
Description	The customer called the help-desk and reported that e-mail is not working, and the help-desk did a password reset.	The customer utilizing his e-mail account to send and receive e-mails
Intangibility	The customer did not see the activities of CPU execution of password reset but witnessed the outcome: the password is now working.	The customer did not see the network and CPU activities but saw the outcome—e-mail display.
Heterogeneity	The help-desk agent's style of communication, language, positive and negative reaction, skills and understanding of service, tools to reset the password, communication/phone system etc. are the heterogeneous components, and each is capable of impacting the experience of the customer.	Reliability and performance of the e-mail server, network, and underlying infrastructure and how people are administering and managing it has direct impact on the customer experience.
Real Time	The help-desk agent is helping the customer, and the customer is realizing the assistance at the same moment.	As soon as the customer invokes his e-mail client and logs in, he is in consumption mode in real time.

Service Characteristic	Help-Desk Service	E-Mail Service
Perishability	For the period of time the customer called the help desk, a set of activities were being performed by the agent at that moment of time, and you cannot store time.	For the period of time the customer was logged in, a set of activities were being performed by the mail's server polling for customer's command to send or receive—even if the customer did not send or receive any e-mail. Those actions cannot be rolled back.

Table 1: Service delivery and support characteristics

3.3   IT Service Factory

A factory by definition is a place for producing a uniform product, without concern for individuality. I would like to apply this definition in the IT service area and consider data centers as IT service factories. This comparison will help us to grasp the concept of service management practices and set our thinking in the correct direction. IT infrastructure thus becomes the manufacturing machineries. Server, application, and system maintenance become the machinery maintenance. Therefore, if people are doing application maintenance, server administration, etc., they are not really producing any service.

The raw material is indeed the data and unprocessed information. The end product is processed information for specific business purposes. The refined end product is also knowledge (and consequential business wisdom).

Data networks (LAN and WAN) are the delivery channels for delivering the end product to the users (service consumers). These channels are also the supply channel for receiving raw material. Analogously, you do have factories to manufacture consumer products as well as customize products to specific customer orders.

So if I remove the word *individuality* from the original definition of factory, I can consider the IT service desk also as a support factory. An IT service desk is a customized product factory where each customer calls with a specific order. Their requests/issue/problems become raw material. Service-desk agents' knowledge and intelligence becomes the production machinery, with auxiliary tools supporting the function of that machinery. The resolutions and request fulfillment becomes the end product. You also have a "return policy," where you rework and rebuild the product (solution) if it does not match with customer's order. There is also a "warranty," whereby a customer can expect further service if a solution no longer performs as expected within a specified period of time.

In both of the above scenarios, ITSM processes become the manufacturing processes. The set of processes do of course have variations, as we see in the next section's discussion of service delivery processes and service support processes.

3.3.1 IT Service Delivery vs. IT Service Support

IT **service delivery** refers to the kind of service where there is no direct interaction between the service producer and service receiver. Services are produced by machines and delivered to receivers via network channels on the receivers' devices. Of course, there are people at both ends. At the service-production end, people operate the machines that produce the service. At the receiver end, a person interacts with his or her device to use the service. Thus,

IT service delivery is machine-to-machine interaction, with a person behind the machine at each end.

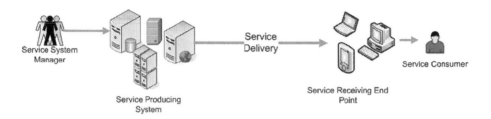

Figure 1: Service Delivery Picture

In ITIL V2, availability management, capacity management, and service-level management processes are key service delivery processes.

As we can see illustrated above, machines perform the prime activity of service delivery, and people (service providers) manage those machines. Machines interface with the customer, with people in background.

This situation gives relatively clear definitions of standards and targets. Processes of production can be effective and leave little scope of deviation from written specifications. The quality is relatively easy to define and achieve. The quality of this aspect of service is **technical quality:** measuring *what* customer was left with when the service was delivered.

A major part of SLAs is devoted to define these aspects of services, because these are definable. Also much of the service-level management activities are focused on this aspect because they are do-able.

The complexity is related to the technology and hard skills that are required for quality delivery. The quality dimensions are reliability, efficiency, performance, completeness, integrity, fault tolerance, and tangibility.

Service support refers to the kind of service where there is a direct interaction between the service provider and service receiver. This need usually arises when the service receiver is not able to use the service. Inability to use does not necessarily mean the service is not delivered. Support will enable the user. If service delivery is interrupted, service support will be a catalyst to restore the service delivery.

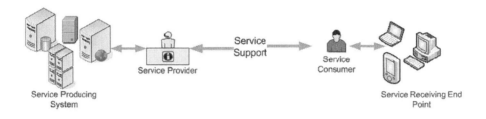

Figure 2: Service Support Picture

In ITIL V2, incident management, problem management, and change management are key service-support processes.

People perform the prime activity of service support, and the customer directly receives the benefit. Here people are dealing with people, and machines are in the background.

This is indeed a complex situation from a standards and definition point of view. Consistency is extremely difficult because of many uncontrollable factors. The quality of service is determined by human factors. Since the human factors exist on both sides (service provider and receiver), the dependency on the human factor is extremely high. Standardization is much harder to achieve. In other words, there is a significant scope of deviation from subjective definitions.

The quality of such aspect of service is the **functional quality**—measuring *how* the customer received the service. The complexity is all about human behaviors, and soft skills are extremely important to accomplish quality service. The quality dimensions governing this aspect of service are responsiveness, courtesy, communication, understanding customers, confidentiality, and emotional resonance.

Traditionally only a part of SLA is devoted to this aspect, and proportionately service-level management activities are just managing to do justice, despite being in a disadvantageous position. The prime processes in this aspect of service are incident management, problem management, and change management. And of course, the service desk is the most important as well as the most visible function encompassing the entire service support system.

As mentioned above, the quality is dependent upon human factors on both sides, and if anything is erratic, that is the human factor. This does imply the following:

1. Service cannot be delivered exactly in the same way repeatedly, because at the core of this is the moment of interaction between two humans.

2. Even if by any method the service could be delivered repeatedly in exactly the same manner, the perception of service quality will differ, because the perception of different customers would not be the same.

3. It is nearly impossible to maintain a consistent service quality in large-scale service support operations.

4. The customer does influence the quality of service.

3.3.2   Transaction-Based Service vs. Perpetual Service

All the services that can be identified, isolated, and contained in a specific instance are referred as transaction-based services. Characteristics of transaction-based services are listed below:

1. Ticket-based

2. Finite life cycle

3. Repetitive instances of same process via different transactions

4. Integral status tracking and easy measurements

5. High visibility

Services delivered as "support" services are usually transaction-based. That means each "piece" of service is measured by a transaction. The most prominent examples of this are IMAC (install, move, add, change) requests (service requests) and incident-resolution service. Other prominent processes to manage this kind of service are event management, change management, and problem management. A customer requests a particular service item. The service providers deliver that particular service item, and the transaction closes.

Perpetual services are, on the other hand, continuously running streams of services, and you tap them when you need them. Examples of this service are web services and e-mail services. The major difference between these two is the service-management process and corresponding measurements. Transaction-based services are normally measured from an elapsed time or duration perspective, while perpetual services are measured from availability and throughput criteria. Service delivery processes, such as availability-management processes and capacity-management processes, are meant for perpetual services.

One of the processes the customer faces in the IT world is service-catalog management, which contains both transaction-based and perpetual services. The service catalog is a document that contains all the services that are provided, a description of the service, service levels, cost of the service, the customer, and the person/department responsible for the maintenance of the service. The content of a service catalog will vary, depending on the requirements of the IT organization.

Service specification sheets often form part of the service catalog. The service catalog includes service delivery aspects as well as service support aspects.

Full-Service Catalog	
Service Catalog	**Service Request (SR) Catalog**
Full set of IT services' supporting business processes	Usually IMAC services for end-user environment
Service catalog includes "perpetual" services also: E-mail service Videoconferencing service	Service request catalog contains services that are one-time transactions: Increase my mailbox quota Install software on my desktop
Difficult to do costing	Easy to do costing
Difficult to build and maintain service catalog	Easy to build and manage SR catalog
Associated SLAs are about availability and performance (e.g., transaction time).	Associated SLAs are about response and resolution time.

Table 2: Service catalog vs Request catalog

3.4. IT Service Complexity

IT service quality depends on who provides the service and when and where the service is provided. For example, e-mail service provided by corporations to their employees will be different if the service is received within the office premises over the LAN or off-site over the WAN. My e-mail will download faster in the office but slower in remote locations, even though the mail server and accounts are the same. As in support services, the capability of the person providing the support will make the difference. Service providers must understand the attributes of the service being provided and ensure that they have people with the right skills for the job. For example, a technically strong person may not be as good as a soft-skilled person for help-desk services. Many IT services depend heavily on people for delivery, and, as human beings are different in skills and nature, consistency cannot be guaranteed. For example, you have standardized your entire desktop environment. Each desktop has the same hardware and software configurations. So each desktop is capable of providing the same service; however, each user uses it in a different manner and derives a different service. Each user will also produce a unique problem, depending on the way he or she uses the desktop environment. Yet another example I have seen regards the iPhone. I use an iPhone but do not use more than five applications. But I consider my problems are more complex, because I have my specific needs.

How to define and manage IT service

IT organizations too often define their services in terms of their capabilities rather than what their customers want as a service. From a customer perspective, four basic components constitute a service:

Elements: Elements are the basic features that a customer expects as part of the service. A service may contain one or more service elements. Each element is described by attributes that characterize that element. Element is depicted by an "included" statement in the service agreement.

If we illustrate help-desk service, then typical elements would include such descriptions as "single point of contact" and "call life-cycle management."

Attributes: Attributes also provide the basic characteristic of an element and direction of service measurements and targets. These are often the part of SLAs.

Continuing with the previous illustration, typical attributes of help-desk service would be hours of operation, channels to contact (e-mail, phone, etc.), life-cycle time (response time, for example) etc.

Deliverables: What customer is left with when service was delivered are called deliverables. This is the main result or output of the service that the customer receives. A clear definition of deliverables helps to define the service scope. This is the end product, and quality parameters do apply here.

In the same illustration, the resolution of the issue or the answer to the question is the deliverable.

Price/Benefit: Price is the payment the service provider expects in return for providing the service. Benefit is the gain the customer realizes because of the service.

Continuing on the same illustration, the gain will be the user productivity and enablement of the user to do his/her work. The price may be based on per call or agreed cost model.

How to tune customer requirements and provider capability

It is very difficult for customers to express real service requirements and performance needs. On the other hand, it is also difficult for providers to differentiate services and tune to specific customers. There are stated and unstated needs. SLAs(Service Level agreements) only focuses on the stated needs. People are inclined to think that the achievement of required service levels will produce customer satisfaction, but that is not true.

Service culture has impact

Service culture is an integrated pattern of value, attitude, practices, goals, beliefs, and behaviors acquired by service provider staff as employees of the organization. This is directly related to working style and therefore the services offered. While a lot of HR guidance is available on developing a service culture within the organization, it is important to note that for service support, organizational culture alone may not be sufficient. It is also inherited from the society, region, and country.

Equality vs. hierarchy paradigm

One of the working-style paradigms in service culture is hierarchy vs. equality. You may find that the tendency to serve according to a hierarchy is more predominant in many Asian cultures; therefore, the personal service rendered by Asians is likely to be better. This is because of a specific working paradigm in Asian culture, in which a hierarchical orientation places a high value on the prevailing power structure and emphasizes the power and status differences among individuals. You follow lines of authority to accomplish the work. Power and status has privileges. This paradigm is prevalent in much of Asian society. Since the customer is deemed to have more authority, there is a natural urge to serve. Whatever the customer desires, the service provider attempts to deliver, regardless of the service contract, because the tendency in a hierarchical structure to fall in line below the authority is natural.

An equality orientation minimizes the power structure in an organization and emphasizes the equality of status among individuals. You are uneasy about formality or use of office titles. You expect that everyone is included and has the same opportunity. This paradigm is prevalent in Western society.

In the equality vs. hierarchy paradigms, the USA, UK, and Germany are highly inclined toward equality, while India and Japan are highly inclined toward hierarchy. Surprisingly, China is in the middle, and France is inclined toward hierarchy.

Since all these are personal orientations of culture, they impact the service support quality, because people deliver these services to people. However, these inclinations do not impact service-delivery quality, which is composed of a people-to-machine relationship.

Universal vs. particular paradigm

Another cultural inclination is about universal vs. particular. Universalistic people place a high value on standards, procedures, rules, and laws. Rules and laws are considered more important than personal relationships. Particularistic people place a high value on the difference and uniqueness of individuals and groups. Standards, procedures, rules, and laws are applied to these individuals on a case-by-case basis. Relationship and social obligations triumph over rules or law. In this cultural inclination, Germany and USA are more universal, while China is the most inclined toward the particular. Surprisingly, France and India are in the middle. This cultural inclination impacts both service delivery and service support.

In global organizations, the cultural traits are getting mixed up, and therefore these differentiations will not be as remarkable as in local organizations.

Thought leadership is not the natural instinct in several cultures that are universalistic, because of the individuals in those cultures having a natural tendency to be followers rather than leaders.

Since support services are produced by people's actions and their mind-sets, we can deduce that the quality of service will also have an impact on social conditions. There are methods and techniques to eliminate the negative effects, which we'll discuss next.

3.4.1 IT Service Quality Gaps

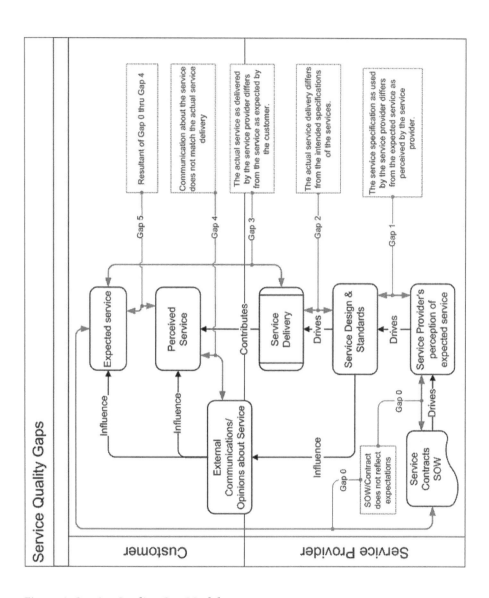

Figure 3: Service Quality Gap Model

Service is interaction and exchange between two parties: namely, the service receiver and service provider. Therefore, the service quality should be solely influenced by the actions and exchanges between these two parties. However, in service quality gaps, you will notice the influence of third parties that have no business in the service transactions also impacts the service quality and introduces the gaps. This influence is because of direct and indirect communication about the services that sets the customer's expectations. For example, I heard great things about a long-distance phone-service provider from my friend and opted to go for it. I was not satisfied because my expectations were set by my friend, who was not an authorized promise-maker for the service provider. The brand value of the provider also provokes some buyer expectations.

The gap really starts with the contractual statement of work (SOW) at the foundation. SOW may not truly reflect the expectations of the customer, and also SOW may not provide the expectation parameters to the service provider, leaving these parameters open for interpretation. Since SOW drives the service provider's perception of expected service, deficiency on the SOW on the expected service sets the foundation of further gaps. Many times the service provider prepares to deliver extraordinary things and delivers them "ordinarily," and the customer is still not excited because the end result is ordinary. Service providers may miss the point that the customer is expecting ordinary things but "extraordinary" delivery. I have seen SOW describing the implementation of a financial-management process for IT service. While the service provider thought of implementation cost models and the charge-back system, the customer was expecting "timely submission of error-free invoices" as the outcome. The SOW design approach is for contract arbitration rather than for relationship-building, and this is one of the weaknesses in operation. An important point to note here is that the customer is an equal partner in setting the foundation of the gap. This has referred as Gap 0 in the diagram 3 above.

Once SOW is finalized, a service provider develops the standards and sets the service delivery systems (people, process, tools, etc.) based on those standards.

Many times the standards are already defined and accounted for while developing the SOW. The service provider thinks that the standards to design the service are based on the SOW and therefore will deliver the expected service, but the standards and design may not be adequate. The service specification as *used* by the service provider differs from the expected service as *perceived* by the service provider. This is referred to as Gap 1 in service quality in the diagram 3 above.

When some inadequate specifications of service management system, process, tools, functions etc. are designed, service providers use those specifications to produce the service. This is the source of Gap 2, as shown in the diagram above. Gap 2 is purely because the system failed within the service provider domain. When actual service delivery starts that is based on the designs and standards, the implementation and adoption of those standards and methodologies are transferred from an actual standard of design on paper. There is always a difference between what you intend to do and what you actually do, primarily because of imperfections in tools and inadequacy of training people. For example, say a customer was expecting 99.9% availability of service, but the system was not designed to serve that purpose—or, if the customer was expecting the issue to be resolved at the first call, but the service desk agent was not trained in the technology needed to resolve the issue.

Even if all the things went right till this point, the actual service delivered by the service provider may differ from the service expected by the user. The contract or SOW may not have any bearing on expectations. For example, say the SLA was three days to install the software; you designed your system and trained people to complete the installation in three days, but the customer was expecting installation in two days. This is an example of Gap 3, as shown in the diagram above. If the service provider does not do anything to set the customer's expectation, the expectation will be set by the customer.

Before, during, and after service rendering, there is regular communication between the service provider and the service receiver. Most often these are overstated and tall claims about the capabilities and feedbacks and do not match with actual service delivery. There are also external communications that are not usually authorized communications about the services: for example, the marketing campaign of competitors against the service provider. These communications influence the perception of the customer as well. Many times service providers alter their designs to come in line with market trends. All these factors produce Gap 4, as shown in the diagram above.

The resultant sum of all the gaps is Gap 5 (as shown in the diagram above), and that gap stems from all false perceptions and expectations combined. Both perceptions and expectations are very difficult to measure and thus make perfection in the service industry seemingly impossible.

3.4.2 Processes to Close the Gaps

Gap 0 is the foundation of all the gaps, even though the Gap 5 is the resul of all gaps and occurs because of one of the most intangible factor for measurement: perception. Preparation of SOW/contracts is usually dominated by legal professionals who are not the actual users or deliverer of services, and, if the stronger participation does not come from the service provider and consumer, there will always be a risk of setting a foundation of future gaps. Since customers drive SOW, and the contracts are driven by the customers, customers unknowingly set up the foundation of service-quality gaps.

By translating customer-service expectations into clear service agreements, Gap 1 can be closed. In ITSM process terminology, you will need strong service-design processes, especially service-catalog management, service-level management, capacity management, and availability management.

Once a comprehensive service agreement is in place, proceed toward using that agreement as a basis for planning and implementing the service delivery.

In an ITIL context, this is the service transition process: namely, service asset and configuration management, service validation, and testing and evaluation. Next, ensure that service delivery and support is done according to planning and procedures. These plans and procedures are covered in the ITIL service operation process set. Finally, manage the configuration about the service delivery via a governance process to close Gap 4. These processes are included in the service strategy and the continual service improvement process (CSIP) of ITIL.

3.4.3 Complexity because of Intangibility

Perception of the service becomes very critical because of the intangibility of the service. Services are not always what they seem to be, and what they *seem* to be is the perception. Since the sum of service-quality gaps converges on perception, it becomes an extremely important aspect in service management. There is very little guidance available on this in the ITSM world (maybe because ITSM is dominated by technology).

Perception management is used with positive or negative ethics and prominent everywhere, from marketing campaigns to diplomacy. When associated with negative ethics, it can also be called propaganda, and it focuses on concealing the truth from the general view to gain benefits by distorting perceptions of reality. An average person is usually compliant and accepting rather than challenging and critical. This allows the continuation of bad works by making them seem like good works.

However, perception management has positive ethics also. The service provided must prominently expose and project the positive aspects of the service quality very actively to create a positive perception. If not, the default perception is likely to be disadvantageous to the service provider. The service provider should prevent presumption and bias from substituting for judgment and reason.

Managing customer satisfaction by perception management

While the IT industry is leading in developing new products and services, it is seriously lagging on the score of customer satisfaction. In other industries the focus has been steadily shifted from product to customer satisfaction, and those efforts are visible in advertisements, publications, and practices. Fortunately the IT industry has realized, at least lately, the importance of perception management, and IT service management that focuses on this subject has started evolving.

It is indeed realistic and possible to achieve higher customer satisfaction by working around customer expectations and perceptions of service quality. This approach takes advantage of the fact that a customer is more readily prepared to criticize bad service than to appreciate good service. This realization is gaining ground in the agenda of current practice of service-level management that has been hitherto more focused on service delivery via hard skills. This shift in focus is justified, because customer dissatisfaction produced by not meeting basic needs is more hurtful than not meeting SLA. Yet for full satisfaction, it is now very important to focus on customer expectations as well.

Perception management involves continuously testing performance against customer expectations and needs, without any formal agreement. This process is based on the measurement of performance and perception and can dynamically calibrate customer expectations.

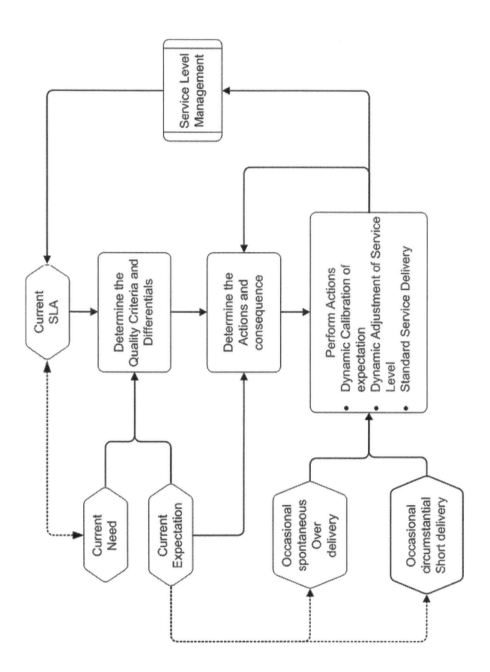

Figure 4: Perception Management

While the above diagram is self-explanatory, it is important to understand that success requires the customer to be a part of the service-provider organization—a stronger bond than the traditional partnership. In simplest terms, it is the successive elimination of high nuisance factors against quality based on customer perception in each iteration of actions.

Prerequisites are as follows:

1. The customer and service provider should have a sense of respect and equality. An attempt to dominate will ensures failure.

2. The consensus culture should prevail with all the parties involved.

3. Understanding each other's point of view is very important.

Take a real-life example for one of the quality criteria of "timeliness" of service: A user reports some printer issue and is unable to print a report. The SLA for resolution of such incident could be eight hours, but the customer's need is four hour, because he or she has to submit a report. The expectations of the user may be two hours because of external factors. So we have three different resolution time targets - SLA of eight hours, need of four hours and expectation of two hours) Following are the possible scenarios:

1. You are targeting the SLA. You resolved the issue in eight hours. You met the SLA, but you did not meet the expectation, nor did you meet the current need.

    a. This *will* result in customer dissatisfaction and a negative image of nonperformance.

    b. This will place you in a disadvantageous position for future transactions of service support.

2. At a service desk, you are aware of the customer's needs and SLA, and you can evaluate the impact of not meeting the need. You decide for over-delivery on this occasion. You resolve the issue in four hours even though the SLA for resolution is eight hours. You meet the need and SLA but not the expectations.

a. This *may* result in customer dissatisfaction but will not place you in a disadvantageous position for future service support.

3. After understanding the expectations, and knowing the need and the SLA as well, you will most probably dynamically negotiate and recalibrate the expectation to what you can deliver. Say you reset the expectations to four hours, and you decide for over-delivery for this occasion and resolve the issue in less than four hours.

a. This will result in customer satisfaction. Yet it may not give you any advantage of future service support.

Important point no note here is that the despite the over delivery with respect to SLA in second scenarios, you are still carrying the risk of customer dissatisfaction.

Guidelines for over-delivery

Each part of service level is usually carries some standards and/or SLA and thus some contractual obligations for the service provider. Under-delivery will not be acceptable to the customer, and over-delivery will not be viable for the service provider, as higher service standards and service levels demand more resources and are an expensive affair.

If you over-deliver, ensure that this over-delivery is occasional only and does not become a routine practice. Also, you must ensure that customers are cognizant of over delivery with respect to SLA or sometimes with respect to need but definitely do not fall in the trap of over delivery with respect to unrealistic expectations. Apart from an economic disadvantage (that you are leaking the possible revenue of higher service levels), over-delivery also sets the expectations of the customer for higher service levels that are not sustainable. Whenever you decide to make an over-delivery, make it loud and clear to customer that it was an exception, so that the future expectations are rightly set.

An occasional short delivery with calibration of customer expectation will not hurt you, so long as you meet the need. In the above example, if the customer's need was twelve hours, the SLA was eight hours, customer expectation was also eight hours, and you resolved the issue in ten hours after dynamically negotiating the expectation to ten hours, you breached the SLA, but you will still achieve customer satisfaction for that transaction. However, if you make such things routine, you will have a dissatisfied customer.

3.4.4 Gaps Originating from Outsourcing Service Contracts

Earlier I talked about service-quality gaps and referred to the SOW as one source of gaps. Now I will explain the flaw that introduces the gap.

Remote Infrastructure Management (RIM) is a commonly outsourced service. Organizations are spending a lot of time, effort, and money to select the right outsourcing vendor and establish a contract.

The customer requests that the managed-service provider provide complete IT infrastructure management, only because the customer has reached a situation where he alone cannot manage his IT efficiently and effectively. The most likely root cause is the customer's chaotic state of ITSM processes because of absence of ITSM architecture and not because of low technical skills. Often business grows, but IT processes cannot scale up. Everyone does their own thing and ends up with different kinds of policies and procedures that lead to individual groups working independently in isolation without adequate collaboration (this structure is most commonly known as silos of towers in IT organization) and that explode costs. The customer chooses outsourcing to drive out these costs. Although there is an alternate option of cost reduction by improving the process and productivity, but that is not explored.

Typically, the error starts from the structure of Request for Proposal (RFP) and RFP response itself. An absolute clarity on vendors' roles about "managing technology" vs. "managing end to end service" is often missing. While the vendor's intent may be to go for managed service, RFP documents dictate the task-level requirements that customers want service providers to do. Ideally, in managed-service outsourcing, the customer should specify the results to be achieved (in terms of SLA) rather than tasks to be performed. Besides this, these tasks are usually an incomplete list and do not form the complete process. These tasks are more often listed for technology management and thus do not guarantee the production of the expected service and service levels. And the problem does not end here; there is another contradiction: the customer specifies, without any condition, both the task and the result. The fact is that the tasks do not produce results; it is the processes that produce the result. Therefore, if those tasks are not logically connected in a well-defined process, the desired result may not be achieved. Often managed-service providers undertake the services on an "as is" process basis. If customers' employees (despite good knowledge of their environment) could not manage their IT with their processes, how can vendors manage with the same processes and with less knowledge about their environment? Since the outsourcing service provider delivers the price advantage for executing tasks, the deal looks good on paper. However, soon these kinds of services turn out to be a "mess for less" proposition. This is a result of mixing responsibility with accountability—or, rather, not differentiating them in the context of task and process. The same fault is repeated, but the customer changes at each occasion. This reminds me of Albert Einstein's definition of insanity: "doing same thing again and again and expecting a different result."

In my view, if it is task outsourcing, then the vendor is responsible for deliverables, and the customer remains accountable for the result. In other words, it is the process that defines outcomes; therefore, the owner of process would always be accountable.

There are several things that the customer wrongly expects from an outsourced vendor. Frequently referred-to expectations are around transformation and value addition that we have discussed in this book's introduction. Yet another expectation is around thought leadership. Where is the scope of thought leadership in task outsourcing?

There are a lot of sourcing advisory and consulting companies who are paid hefty amounts by customers who are seeking to outsource their IT infrastructure management and/or application management. These consulting companies are experts in guiding and managing the vendor selection process using their methods but still fail to differentiate between technology management and service management. In fact, they repeat the same faulty concept of dictating the tasks but expecting the result.

3.4.5 Other factors

More and more service production activities will be transferred to the consumers themselves. Airlines are quite advanced in this area. Passenger check-in, for example, is largely handled by machine and the passenger himself. Now consumers themselves transfer money or perform several account-management services in banks. In the IT industry, the new models of services namely infrastructure as a service (IaaS), platform as a service (PaaS) and software as a service (SaaS) are fully delivered by machines. Although the service provider promises to keep in mind the usability aspect and maintain user friendliness, there is a limit to the extent a machine can understand the degree of naïveté (or sophistication) of individual consumers and accordingly recalibrate the system in real time. Therefore the caliber of the service consumer will also be a factor that will determine the quality of service. For example, an expert user will be able to obtain more value from an automated system that is producing a service than will an average user, who will draw less service from the same system. The limit is not the service-delivery capability nor the appetite to consume the service but the ability to obtain the value from this kind of delivery.

The production of support service is also being automated, although to a lesser extent, because at some point you must provide consumers access to a live person. Support brings in value for consumers with less knowledge or sophistication, but that support will be more expensive. This cost will tend to lessen the value or profit incentive for the company to provide the service as the value of the service is inversely proportional to the cost of service.

4 SIGNIFICANCE OF PROCESSES

Business and manufacturing industries long ago realized that business and manufacturing processes, and not the people or technology, are the keys to error-free performances. The same hypothesis can be expanded to state that service-management processes are the key to error-free IT service delivery. The IT industry has yet to get fully convinced of this; although ITIL, the process-led approach, made that attempt, most of the IT organizations are still attempting to solve process problems with tools.

The obvious is often not very easy to see (rather, people do not want to see it), despite realizing that most service problems could not be corrected by technology configurations. IT operation management's job should be to develop the processes, and staff should just work within their boundaries. Unfortunately, people are left to work with their own processes. When crisis occurs, everyone works hard and ultimately solves the problem that created the crisis. If the processes were right, the problem will be prevented in the first place.

A lot has been said about service-quality improvement with various methods. While quality is about delivering service right every time, the process goes a step beyond that: it brings in the perfection, and that is delivering the right level of service every time.

IT organizations can no longer survive by pouring in more people and more technology to improve quality and defeat the competition. They need to completely restructure service-management processes. I have often seen two common mistakes:

1. Tool implementation is regarded as processes implementation: this, in fact, is the victory of vendors' propaganda that out-of-the-box implementation brings in the best practice.

2. Even where tools are used to automate processes, the process is still amateur. By automating bad processes, we only ensure that we do a bad job more quickly and with less effort.

At this time I would just list some of the benefits of adopting the process-led approach for service management, with a brief indicative logic to support each example of how this approach can help your organization. As you complete this book, you should be able to derive the detailed and logical explanation of how you can benefit by implementing a process-led approach to service.

Focusing on the customer: Every process has a primary goal that is linked, directly or indirectly, with some specific customer purpose. For example, the goal of incident-management process is to restore the service as soon as possible. This is direct customer focus. The goal of problem management is to identify and eliminate the weakness in infrastructure—indirectly a huge contribution to customer purpose. A process-led approach by default leads to customer focus.

Predicting and controlling changes: A well-designed process defines internal and external Key Performance Indicators (KPIs). These KPIs provide the pattern of output and results with various forms of inputs. Logical work-flow acts as an algorithm of the process that can be extrapolated to predict the next step and control the outcome. For example, in a well-designed capacity management, you can predict the seasonal demand and control the consumption of services.

Improving the utilization of available resources: process consumes resources, and, during an initial design, resource optimization is one of the design criteria. Continual improvement and streamlining also addresses the resource optimization. For example, a well-defined batch-job management process will significantly improve the capacity utilization of computing resources.

Preventing the error: Highly matured processes make the service production a matter of procedural task executions. Work instruction within the process makes the outcome more deterministic. Mature processes are, by design, repeatable, and repeatability of proven processes prevents errors.

Providing the view of how an error occurred and how to correct it: There is a built-in tracking mechanism of the tasks and actors, or agents, along with the control feedback. This allows you to trace and correct errors.

Providing the complete measurement of the system: Processes generate a variety of data for internal as well as external consumption. These data points feed into the measurement system.

Controlling the entropy of IT organization: Policies and guidelines surrounding the process are built-in controls to control the entropy or disorder. (We will further discuss the term *entropy* later in section 4.6 as the degree of disorder in a service-management environment.)

Process is the most critical instrument for service governance: Governance is about the right people making the right decisions, and process measurements greatly facilitate that. They allow you to make decisions based on what you know rather than what you think. (Later in this book in Chapter 11 I will talk about how processes support IT governance.)

Effectively managing relationships between groups in an IT organization: A process defines the task input and output exchange point, establishing protocol among the actors, who are usually spread across different departments or different organizations. These protocols eliminate disputes and enable application actors to work toward the same goal.

4.1 Process Thinking

If IT is deemed to be a business, then it ought to be process-driven. Think of your data center as the service-manufacturing factory where you deploy lots of machineries to produce the IT service and deliver that service via network pipes to the service consumers at their port. You may use a telecom distributor and pay delivery charges.

The process-driven organization will bring in radical change in thinking and approaches toward problem-solving and conducting the business. Some examples follow:

Employees making mistakes vs. the process allowing mistakes

In a process paradigm, a general approach is to establish a proven process (and of course keep it proven all the time through a process-management function). Once a process is established, identify the actor roles and assign them to appropriate employees. It is assumed that role-players will be adequately trained (which is a part of process implementation). The onus of producing the result is thus primarily shifted to the process, and, in case of deviation from the expected result, the first check should be on the process rather than on the employee. Take, for example, an incident in which a change-management process implementer performed a change assigned to him, without any approval. What was the problem? The change was deemed "standard," which does not require any approval as per policy—but it was not really a standard change. Also, the Request for Change (RFC)is assigned for implementation implies that it is clear for implementation. Thus there are two problems—first, there was no validation that the RFC was really "standard RFC" at the time of submission; and second, there was no verification at the time of assignment. The checks were made at the time of completion, which is less logical, as the error had already occurred. The wrong approach here is that checks were applied to detect the error rather than prevent the error. So think: *Are employees the problem, or is process the problem?*

Employees doing the job vs. employees using process to do the job

In many jobs Key Responsibility Area (KRA) and goals are defined for individuals, but those KRA do not fit well into the process roles. Also, while implementing the process, role-mapping is not adequately done. This creates individual silos performing discreet tasks without the context of the whole process. In a perfect world of mature process, it would be okay; however, in real life process relies upon the appropriate use of guidelines, and, if those guidelines are used without the adequate context, the process will fail. For example, in incident-management process, incident-ticket life-cycle management is the responsibility of the service-desk agent, but that does not mean that the service-desk agent is responsible for producing the solution. If this responsibility is not adequately understood, then the agent will be pressured to produce a resolution that may not be correct. So employees not only need to understand their jobs but also *must* know how their jobs fit into the total process.

Measuring individuals vs. measuring processes

We do measure the efficiency and effectiveness of the process by measuring the output that the process delivers. This is similar to what we stated in the first point above. For example, in an incident-management process, there is a lot of value in measuring how much time it took to fix a disruption in service rather than measuring how many tickets an individual resolved.

Motivating people vs. removing barriers

In the process paradigm, we will believe that the failure in producing the result will be because of some barrier in the execution of the process, not because of the low-morale or demotivated employee. (Inspiration is better than motivation.) For example, in a service desk there is a volume of tickets, and backlog is increasing. There are two possible options. You motivate the agents to work harder and take more tickets, or you eliminate the cause of the backlog, such as availability of tools or knowledge base, enabling the faster resolution.

Who made the error vs. what allowed the error to occur

In case of error, the first check should always be made on the error condition surrounding the process policies, guidelines, and tasks. It is quite possible that an operation encounters certain business situations for which the extant process was not originally designed. For example, an incident-management process is designed to receive the request to fix a break in the system and provide resolution. In this process, the request will be received, it will be assigned, and after repair work it will be resolved. What if a request is received for privileged access and handled through the same process?

4.2 Process Compliance and Bureaucracy

Bureaucracy is a management structure within a company. Basically it's a way to manage operations. Usually it evolves within large corporations or the government. The bureaucratic structure is a form of management of operations through departments, managers, and people under them. It's formed to help better manage something, but it can get too bulky and inefficient. Bureaucratic red tape can be common, which is characterized by excessive formality and routine required before official action can be taken.

An organization is deemed bureaucratic when its policies don't satisfy the customer's individual situation; that is, the policies and procedures are rigid and applied uniformly across all situations.

There are two kinds of problems in bureaucracy: namely the negativity related to process and procedures and the negativity related to people and culture

Bureaucracy results from organizational culture or individual personalities and is rooted in the following psychology:

1. Fear of being blamed for wrongdoing—this makes employees create evidence of their right actions in the system, which takes time and effort. This behavior also occurs because of a general mistrust for others as well as for the system.

2. Inadequate training—lack of information and experience about just what tasks requires what actions and under what conditions.

3. Lack of work—employees do not have enough work and want to add steps to a process to justify their existence.

4. Desire to over-control.

5. Desire to maintain monopoly over important information, making employees unwilling to share

6. Not being willing to delegate

The following story is one example of the bureaucracy of the old days.

My father's colleague retired from state government service and was living on a government pension. The pension-disbursement procedure was very straightforward. Every month my father's colleague goes to the listed post office with a certificate to proof he is alive (usually issued by the local government hospital), submits a claim, and attaches the certificate. The pension is then disbursed over the counter. This was working routinely, and everyone was happy—till my father's colleague went for a long trip to Bombay (now Mumbai) to visit his son. He stayed there for three months. After his return, he went to claim his pension for three months: March, April, and May. He submitted the certificate proof of being alive for May and claimed the pension for three months. The clerk disbursed the pension for May but not for March and April, because his proof of being alive was not attached to the claim for those months. His logic was that if a person is alive in May, that is itself evidence of his being alive in previous months—but that reasoning did not work against the rule that the proof must be enclosed with the claim. He had to come back with the required evidence to claim the pension for March and April.

In the next chapter, we will discuss three important components of a process: the policy, rules, and guidelines. The case of my father's colleague is one where policy was treated as the rule. The proof of being alive was the policy that was supported by guidelines of what is admissible proof; however, the person executing those work instructions had carved them in stone. It may be that the problem was that of an individual not adequately trained to follow the intent of the guideline and ending up following the self-developed rigid rule.

It is also possible that a policy might have been really rigid and illogical. In that case I will call it an unmanaged process. The process is not being maintained—the inconsistencies and deficiencies of the process are not being corrected.

It may seem that the bureaucracy is negative all the time. But I believe that bureaucracy has some advantages:

1. Transparency and openness

2. Clear norms and rules

3. Predictable outcome

4. Defined accountability

Process compliance has all these advantages, and, by virtue of flexibility and judged, evaluated performance, all the disadvantages of bureaucracy are eliminated.

4.2.1 Self-Serving Process

There are many tasks built into a process. Ideally each task should have some purpose toward the end goals of the process, but that would not be the case all the time. Several tasks are built within a process that does not serve the purpose of the end customer but rather serves some internal purpose; for example, building several steps in an incident-management process to measure OLA (operational-level agreement; i.e., the internal SLA within the service-provider groups). These steps may not improve customer service directly but increase the maintainability of process and provide measurements for improvements. We also add a few steps to collect a variety of data on the way of process execution. This data may not have any relevance to resolution but are for some internal use. These are the process overheads. Overheads decrease the throughput of process and cannot be eliminated—they are a cost of doing business. When the process overheads become overwhelming, the entire process becomes self-serving. The cost of doing business should never bear pressure on the selling cost of services.

4.2.2 Process Maturity

Many organizations obtain certificates of compliance and project that as an evidence of service quality. ISO certification never guarantees quality. It proves only that an organization can deliver a certain quality standard at a specific time. It does not prove that quality standards are really met.

Similarly, there has been lot of focus on process maturity as well. Maturity models are useful as collections of best practices and the stages in which to try to adopt them. They provide profiles of IT processes describing possible current and future states. Substantial amounts of money for research have been spent on maturity models, and they are recognized as a good tool to set the standard for continuous improvement. I strongly believe in the maturity model but would like to make the following notes of caution:

1. Maturity is not automatically a good thing.

2. Maturity is not a goal; it is a characterization of an organization's methods for achieving its core goals.

3. Mature processes impose expenses that must be justified by consequent cost savings, revenue gains, or service improvements.

4. "Immature processes" does not mean "can't do good work." It means "good results depend on whether the company's star performers are doing their jobs," or it is the result of individual heroic performance.

5. Maturity predicts the worst that an organization might do on a job, not the best that it could do.

Therefore maturity scores will provide value only if they are reviewed along with a gap analysis where you analyze the deviation between the actual process and the "should be" process. Ultimately after all maturity assessment and gap analysis, you will fall back on process engineering or reengineering to get the things right. This is similar to someone obtaining training, passing certification examination, and being skilled. A person can obtain training and be skillful even without passing the examination. Of course passing a certification examination provides assurance that the examinee will be skillful. However, certification does not guarantee that this person will be skillful. A certified person may still lack skill. Conversely, a person without certification can have skills. Furthermore, formal training is not necessary to either possess a skill or to pass an examination. Training, examination, and skill possession can be three independent things.

4.2.3 ITSM Process vs. Technical Process

ITSM refers to service management processes that are used to manage IT service and not the technical process to manage technology.

Service management (SM) process covers the generic processes for managing and governing the lifecycle of IT services as produced by IT resources. This is technology-independent and focuses on the work-flow and work-policy aspect of IT service.

IT processes are specific technical processes for the task or activity defined by the SM process and are technology- and product-dependent. Technical processes are covered in product operation manuals and run books and are more procedural technical activities. You can also refer to technical processes as technology- management processes, and I will use this terminology as well further on in this book.

In the following diagram, you can see the relation between ITSM and technical processes. Technology-management (TM) process is always invoked within a service-management process. Multiple TM processes can be invoked within one service-management process. They can be invoked in series or in parallel. One SM process can contain diversified TM process for multiple technologies.

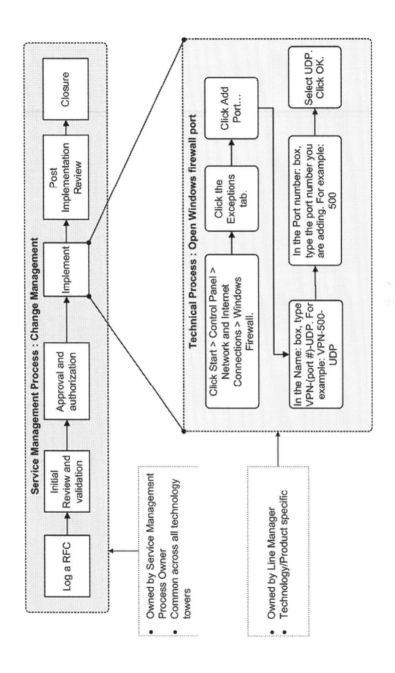

Figure 5: Service management Process Vs Technical Process

Since technical processes are technology-specific, the product and technology vendors have incentive to develop, maintain, and promote best practices around technology. Service-management processes' best practices are developed by technology-independent organizations without any affiliation to technology vendors. Prominent organizations are OGC for ITIL and ISACA for CoBIT. For a good quality of IT service, you need both SM processes and TM processes. However, the scope of this book is confined to service-management processes.

4.2.4 IT Service Composition and Process

Let us examine the span of processes in IT service composition. The model described in the diagram above explains IT service composition. There are three core attributes: utility, warranty, and assets. There are two kinds of assets: one related to resources and another related to capabilities. ITIL covers utility and warranty in detail.

Customers perceive utility based on service attributes that positively affect the performance of tasks associated with desired outcomes. Utility indicates that the service is fit for the purpose. Warranty is derived from the positive effect being available when needed. Warranty indicates that the service is fit for use. The combination of utility and warranty adds value. So a help-desk service has utility when it is providing the resolution service to the customer, and it has warranty if the delivered resolution to the technical issue solves the problem.

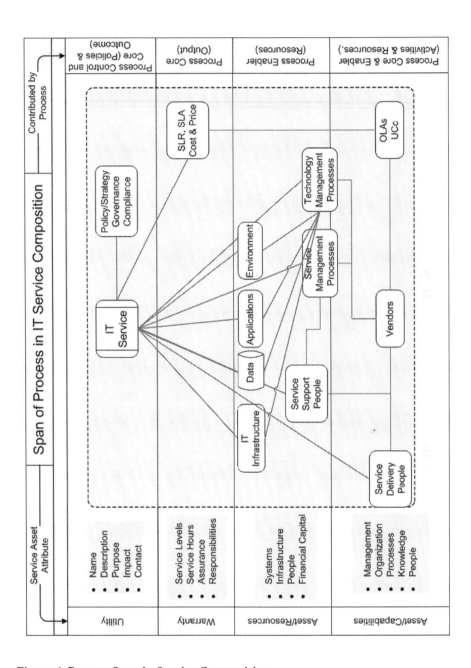

Figure 6: Process Span in Service Composition

As you see in the diagram above, that is based on the service composition model of ITIL, the contribution of process is pervasive in all aspects of IT service composition.

4.3 Process Management

Manage is a very diverse and general-purpose word, but, when used with some object, it means to take care of that object (for example, "managed objects" in the technology world). Thus, process management is the act of taking care of process. This is indeed meaningful if you consider process as an asset that is delivering some value to the business. In order to make this meaning more exhaustive, I will define *process management* as *the art and science of directing human and tool activities that deal with all aspects of process life cycle.* If process is not professionally managed, it will still change, but that will be an unmanaged change. The criteria for this change would be for the convenience of the people in the process rather than for the best interest of the organization or even the customer. Unmanaged process becomes inefficient, ineffective, stale, overly complicated, labor-intensive, time-consuming, and irritating to the customer, employees, and managers. Above all, it also burdens the organization with bureaucracy.

There is a cost to manage process, but the cost of unmanaged process is even higher. The following supposedly hypothetical situation is applicable to all organizations:

Consider the cost of negative impact on user productivity, because a user cannot perform his business function due to a desktop/laptop issue. He gets the issue resolved by the help-desk. Apart from visible time to fix the issue, do you account for the associated time cost that may be because of poor processes—for example, communication time with the help-desk? A good incident-management process can save you much more money than what you spend on implementing and managing it. Consider the following illustrative data: There are ten thousand employees in an organization with business revenue of $5 billion, and the IT help-desk receives five thousand requests per month. The average time spend on communication with the help-desk is ten minutes, and the average time to resolve an issue is twenty minutes. If a good process cuts down the communication time by four minutes per call, the productivity gain would equal over $200,000!

Similarly, a good capacity-management process can avoid panic-buying cost and save millions. (Optimization of capacity leads to avoidance of the 15 percent of extra capacity. Avoid panic buying at an inflated price of 15 percent on an installed base of fifteen hundred servers, with the average cost of server being $10,000, and this saving is $2.25 million!) This is analogous to the fact that there is a cost and effort to remaining healthy, and that is much cheaper than the cost of sickness, even if all your medical costs are fully paid by insurance.

There are three major phases in the process-management life cycle:

1. Process Development: Design deals with policy, guidelines, workflow, rules, roles, responsibilities, and the like. At this stage a design document is created along with the functional specification for the tool in which the process will be enabled.

2. Process Implementation: "Build" is actually the tool implementation, testing, tool deployment, role assignment, training, and so on.

3. Process Operation: "Run" is actually the processes in action. A part of the process will run or be enabled by the tool, and part will be outside the tool. The percentage will vary depending upon the level of automation.

As shown in the figure below, process management deals with the life cycle of process. Process life cycle consists of various phases through which a process moves from beginning to end. These phases are usually grouped into three—development phase, implementation phase, and operation phase. Development includes requirements and design; implementation includes tool/application customization and deployment, while operation includes the run and optimization. As you can see, there is 1:1 ratio in the end-to-end management cycle.

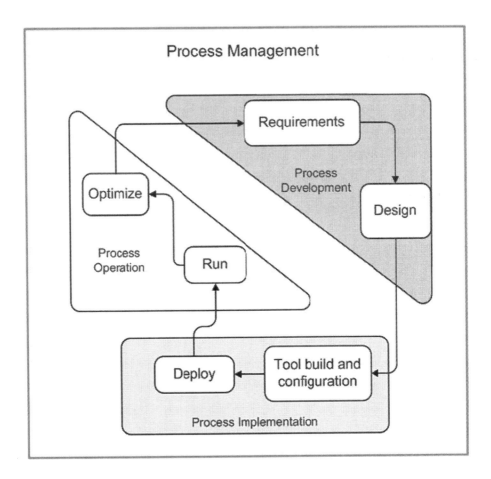

Figure 7: Process Management View

Software-application management

Application management deals with the entire life cycle of an application. An application life cycle consists of various phases through which an application travels from beginning to end. These phases are usually grouped into two—development phase and production phase. Development includes requirements, design, and build, while production includes deploy, operation, and optimize. Although this life-cycle model seems to be linear and water-fall-based, it is perfectly suitable for use in modern system-development approaches such as rapid application development (RAD). It is important to mention that adding features to an existing application or using it in different way does not constitute creating a new application and therefore does not create a new application life-cycle.

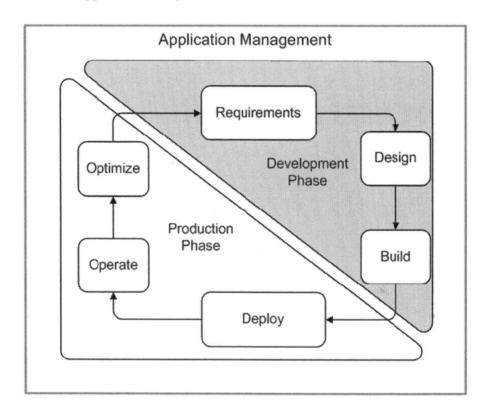

Figure 8: Application Management Overview

Process Management		Application Management	
Phase	Steps	Phase	Steps
Process Development	Requirements	Development	Requirements
	Design		Design
Process Implement	Implement		Build
	Deploy	Production	Deploy
Process Operation	Run		Operate
	Optimize		Optimize

Table 3: Process management and Application management analogy

4.3.1 Process Maintenance

Process is like software and therefore requires maintenance. We all know and understand the importance of software-application maintenance and are willing to pay for it. However, not long ago, when software as a tangible asset was evolving, the concept of software maintenance was missing. The maintenance was perceived to be associated with "wear and tear" and largely applicable to hardware. Now software maintenance is a well-established discipline, and its cost is accounted for. I believe that in the future process maintenance will also be well understood and recognized. The following attributes clarify the analogy between process and software. Both of them

1. need ongoing maintenance,

2. should be upgraded with business needs,

3. can have bugs that should be removed when detected,

4. need training for users to use to full potential/purpose, and

5. must be compatible with other interfacing processes.

A common perception of software maintenance is that it merely involves fixing bugs. However, studies and surveys over the years have indicated that the majority—over 80 percent—of the maintenance effort is used for non-corrective actions. This perception is created by faulty processes in organizations in which users submit problem tickets that in reality are functionality enhancements to the system. The correct meaning of software maintenance in software engineering is the modification of a software product after delivery to correct faults, to improve performance, or to add other attributes.

Analogously, process improvement and enhancement is a larger part of process maintenance than is bug-fixing.

Like software maintenance, process maintenance is also categorized into four classes:

1. Adaptive maintenance—dealing with changes and adapting in the software environment

2. Perfective—accommodating new or changed user requirements that concern functional enhancements to the software

3. Corrective—dealing with errors found and fixing them

4. Preventive—activities aiming to increase software maintainability and prevent problems in the future

Since the concept of process maintenance is rarely understood and practiced, there is a vacuum in the area of formal methods and processes for process maintenance like those we have established and proven in software-maintenance processes and methodologies. Management is more than maintenance, and it includes improvements also.

Analogy with application maintenance

Just as the operation and optimization part of application life-cycle management is regarded as maintenance, the running and optimization part of process is also regarded as maintenance, and the same principles apply that we just saw above. However, the irony in the process-maintenance world is that people do not pay for process maintenance, but they pay for tool maintenance for tools that rarely break.

4.3.2 Process Management Eliminates Bureaucracy

Process management deals with maintaining the process—that is, keeping it current with business needs, identifying the barriers, and eliminating them, thereby streamlining the processes.

The source of bureaucracy is inefficient and ineffective processes.

BUREAUCRATIC APPROACH	PROCESS APPROACH
Strict adherence to rules without consideration of purpose	Purpose driven performance of a defined set of activities
Iron cage of control to pin down accountability	Flexible control within defined boundaries
No empowerment	Empowerment within boundaries
Does not require judgment	Requires judgment
Noncompliance will lead to disciplinary action.	Noncompliance will have an impact on purpose/quality.
Focus is to show that right things were done.	Focus is to do right things.

Table 4: Process vs bureaucracy

4.4 Process vs. Function

Functions are units of organization specialized to perform certain types of work and be responsible for specific outcomes. Functions tend to optimize work methods locally so to focus on the assigned outcome. Poor coordination between functions combined with inward focus leads to functional isolation or silos. The figure below depicts how function and process are related and linked to results.

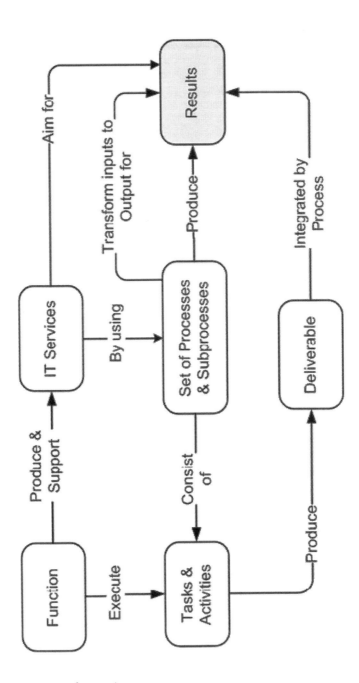

Figure 9: Process and Function

Process is a logical set of connected activities, regardless of function, that perform procedures. Process models help to integrate functional silos. Processes are measurable and aim at specific goals. Process cuts across functions.

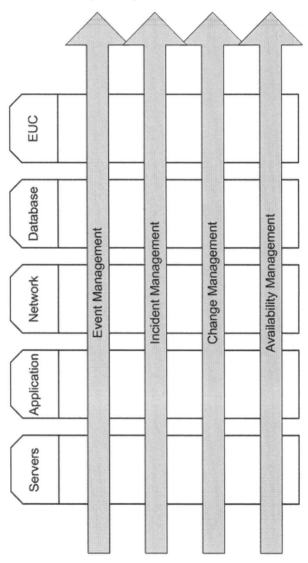

Figure 10: Processes binding isolated departments

While this is a significant change from a traditional, hierarchically managed organization, it will be required to coexist with the traditional lines of management authority.

4.5 Process-Management Maturity Model

In an organization with process management as a recognized function, line-manager-based operation management is typical of any legacy IT infrastructure-based service. As a transition to service management, process-management-based delivery shows how people will align to enable cloud-based delivery.

The process-management maturity model indicates how good the process-management function in the organization is. This function can assume different names, such as service-management office, service-integration tower, and cross-functional service, but the underlying purpose is the same—establish the process ownership and manage the process life cycle.

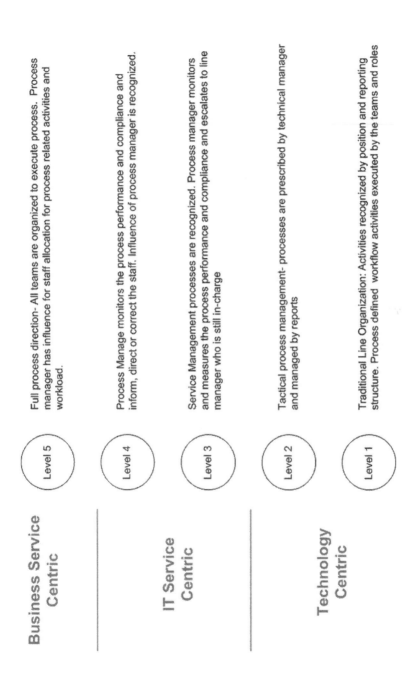

Figure 11: Process Management Maturity

Maturity Level 1

At this level, technology management is deemed to be service management, and specific technical processes are adequately functioning. Maturity level 1 is typical of traditional line organization, where activities are recognized by a position and reporting structure. Individual processes are ad hoc within the technology silo, and defined work-flow activities are executed by various teams with specific roles. Service goals are not clear, and little measurement takes place. Typical traits of an organization at this process-management functional maturity include the following:

- IT is driven by technology, and most initiatives are aimed at trying to understand infrastructure and deal with exceptions.

- Technology management is performed by technical experts, and only they understand how to manage each device or platform.

- Most teams are driven by incidents, and most improvements are aiming at making management easier—not to improve service.

- The organization entrenches technology specialization and does not encourage interaction among groups.

Maturity Level 2

Tactical process management indicates this maturity level—processes are prescribed by a technical manager and managed by reports. Some goal-setting occurs. Some measurements are established but known only to management. There is inconsistent performance-monitoring for system performance. Each technology silo works with its own service-management process that is internally developed. Typical traits of an organization at this process-management functional maturity include the following:

- Initiatives are aimed at achieving control and increasing the stability of technology infrastructure.

- IT has identified most technology components and understands what each is used for.

- Technical management focuses on achieving high performance of each component, regardless of its function.

- Point solutions are used to automate those processes that are in place, usually on a platform-by-platform basis.

- Recognition and need for common processes across all technology silos starts emerging and takes shape in basic processes, primarily the incident and change processes.

- Out-of-the-box tool-implementation mania prevails.

Maturity Level 3

At this level of organizational maturity, service-management processes are recognized. The process manager monitors and measures the process performance and compliance and reports to the line manager, who is still in charge. Some effectiveness goals and measures are set but not adequately communicated. More individual tower-based processes start merging into a unified cross-towered process. Basic SLAs and OLAs are understood, and SLAs are reviewed. Typical traits of organization at this level of process-management functional maturity include the following:

- Critical services have been identified, along with their technological dependencies.

- Systems are integrated to provide required performance, availability, and recovery for those services.

- There is more focus on measuring performance across multiple devices and even platforms.

- Process ownership is assigned but not adequately empowered. Tools dominate process implementation.

Maturity Level 4

At this maturity level, the process manager monitors the process performance and compliance and informs, directs, or corrects the staff. The influence of the process manager is recognized. Effectiveness and efficiency are measured and communicated, as well as linked to service SLA goals. Process is regularly and critically defined, with full support and agreement from technology towers but under the ownership of named process owners. Accountability for this assessment is clear and enforced. Typical traits of an organization at this process-management functional maturity include the following:

- Services are qualified, and initiatives are aimed at delivering appropriate levels of service.

- Service requirements and technology constraints drive procurement.

- Service design specifies performance requirements and operational norms.

- A consolidated system supports multiple services.

- All technology is mapped to services and is managed to service requirements.

- Processes are formally owned and managed with adequate empowerment to process owners. Process owners drive tool implementation.

Maturity Level 5

At this level of maturity, cross-functional service-management process is fully implemented. All teams are organized to execute process. The process manager influences staff allocation for process-related activities and workload.

ITSM processes are kept in sync with business processes, and business-process change triggers the reassessment of process-control capability. Process management regularly performs self-assessment to confirm that processes continue to meet the goals and remain effective and efficient. Process-management functions benchmark the processes to external good practice and seek external advice. Employees across all technology groups are proactively involved in process improvement. All tools used to automate or enable processes are owned and managed by a process-management function. Typical traits of an organization at Level 5 process-management functional maturity include the following:

- IT is measured in terms of its contribution to business.

- All services are measured by their ability to add value.

- Processes are deemed to be assets, and the process owner controls the tool.

4.5.1 A Case for Service-Management Office (SMO)

In order to build a case for SMO, let us discuss the need for service-management architecture. In all IT worlds, we recognize the need for a variety of architectures that includes network architecture, data architecture, application architecture, and system architecture. All these architectures serve the purpose of service, but unfortunately people rarely focus on service architecture and service management architecture. We need service -management architecture for the following reasons:

- IT service costs too much; costs of managing complexity are very high.

- We need to eliminate desperate and redundant efforts in service management.

- We need to deal with a growing IT system for service management.

- We have an ever-increasing rate of change.

- Sharing is more critical for success.

- We need to be ready for multi-vendor service models and outsourcing.

- Future-proofing is required in service-management investments.

So, the need for SM architecture automatically leads to the need for an SMO that will own and manage it, bringing in value through service-management architecture compliance.

Earlier I gave an example of Winchester Mystery House, which was built without any consideration for architecture. Well, in IT operations also, especially in IT service management area, I often come across the similar practice. Organizations build and deploy service management systems without any considerations for architecture. You may call it ad-hoc implementation and of course, it does work. The question is that it is fit for the purpose and fit for the use?

I want to emphasize that managing the technology is not good enough and you need to manage services. And that is where strong service management architecture is needed.

Service Management architecture will help to avoid the mixing of technology service and business service. It will segregate the Technology management with Service Management and establish the services as the manageable entities.

Multivendor service is a common scenario and the service to your customers will demand integration of services from multiple vendors. Managing vendor is not good enough and you need to manage the service from that vendor as a component of your service.

Growing IT Ecosystem and emerging cloud architectures further emphasize the complexity of service management. Vendors will provide tools and method to manage the complexity of their product but Service to your customer is ultimately your product.

Outsourcing is now a routine business model and more often you will outsource services in parts. You will need to manage and integrate those service components.

Architecture also addresses the need of future flexibility and future expandability.

So you establish architecture for service management. But then who will manage the ITSM system and maintain it?

How to establish and operate an SMO

Each organization has a project-management office that directs works under the CIO. I visualize the same concept for an SMO. Organizations that are mature enough to establish and operate project and program-management offices can draw clues from there for establishing a service-management office. The first step in this direction is to establish a charter of SMO organizations that would be based on the needs stated in the list above.

5 PROCESS FUNDAMENTALS

In this section we will talk about the basics of process engineering; before we start on that, we need to establish and clarify some common concepts necessary to understand process engineering.

What is a process?

A process is an activity or a group of activities that receives input: a process can add value and provide some output. The value comes from the purpose or the benefit it adds toward the end goal. Another commonly accepted definition of process is "the logically related series of activities connected toward a defined goal," but I consider that definition inadequate, because a process is more than a set of activities. As we shall learn in subsequent sections, input and output are very significant parts of the process, and I believe they should be mentioned prominently in the definition as well. The input can be a data or a result of another activity, and the output also could be the value-added data or the result of an activity. The major difference is that the input must be tangible, while the output may not be tangible (if it is a service, for example). One example is the knowledge-management process, which takes data as input and converts it into knowledge, which is its output. In this case, there will be multiple tasks; first you will convert data into information and then information into knowledge. In some of the context the knowledge may be intangible, but the input data and the information will always be tangible. Another important aspect is the value addition. The knowledge will always have a higher value than the data or the information, because it is supporting the purpose or producing the benefit toward the end goal of process. In other words, the value from the process will come from the purpose or the benefit that is added by a series of interrelated activities. One task alone performed by one person is not a process.

5.1 Process Hierarchy

One of the basic components of the process is task. A task is an assigned piece of work, often to be finished within a certain time. Tasks may be big and long or small and short, and in some cases can be broken into sub tasks. Sub tasks are ranked at the same level in the process hierarchy and used more for managing and measuring the finer points of the tasks.

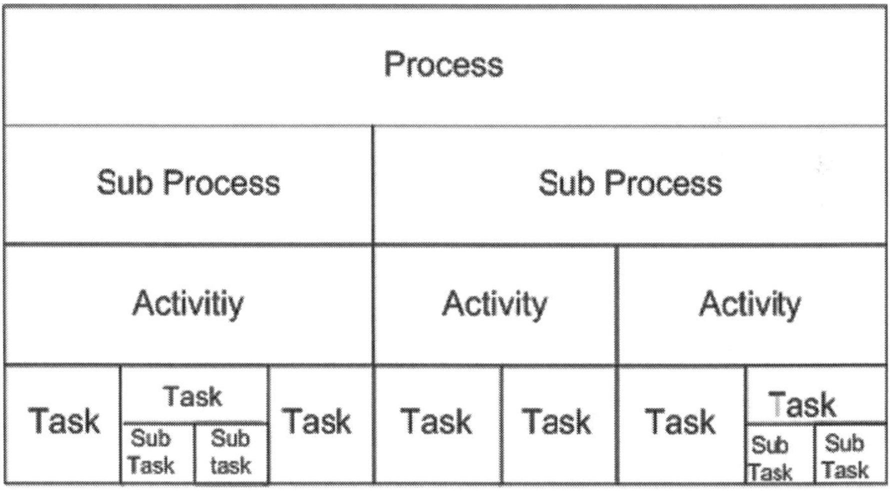

Figure 12: Process, activity and task

At the next level, we do have activity. An activity is a specific deed, action, function, or sphere of actions. Activity is organized as a set of tasks that is measurable. A task may or may not be measurable, but activity can be measured. A measurable task can also be referred as an activity.

Several activities can be grouped to form a sub process or a process itself. This implies that a process can be broken into sub processes or sets of activities.

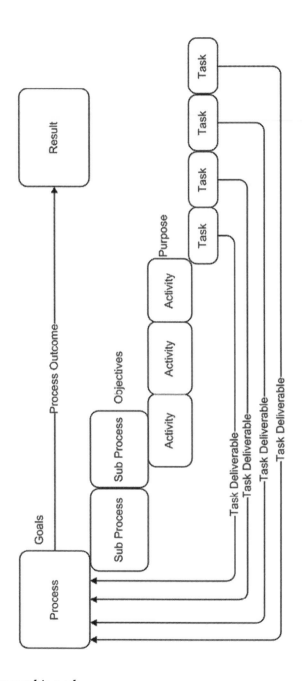

Figure 13: Process hierarchy

It is important to understand that the boundaries between each layer can be blurred and cannot be very well defined all the time. Many times tasks and activities can be used interchangeably. In our process-engineering document, we will refer to them interchangeably. It is, however, very important to have a few points to take away from this discussion:

1. Goals/results/outcome are achieved by virtue of process.

2. Tasks produce some deliverables within the process and compose the process in order to form the output.

3. Sub processes work at an objective level.

4. Activities are defined for a purpose.

It would be worthwhile to establish some related definitions in this subject.

Method

Method is an established, habitual, logical, or prescribed practice or systematic process of achieving certain ends with accuracy and efficiency, usually in an ordered sequence of fixed steps.

It is also interesting to note that ITIL that became popular as "process-led approach" really began as "method." The first version of ITIL that was born in 1980 was officially termed government information technology infrastructure management method—GITIMM.

Practice

Practice is the application of methods, procedures, processes, and rules used in a particular field or profession.

Procedure

Procedure is a sequence of steps to execute a routine activity or task. Procedures prescribe how one should proceed in certain circumstances in order to produce a desired output.

Further, procedure is a documented description of process with the names of the involved parties. Procedures also establish the boundary of judgment required for process compliance.

Policy

Policy is a guide to thinking, action, and decision. Policies can exist at any level, from process level to the lowest level where tasks are executed.

Policy is essentially the documented set of broad guidelines, formulated after envisioning all factors (use cases) that can affect a process. Policy lays down the process response to known and unknown situations and circumstances.

Rules or policies have the potential to alter the work-flow within a process. Process policy may bypass some process tasks or may add some process task—for example, consider a policy statement of a change-management process: "If a Severity 1 outage ticket requires a Change for resolution, then RFC can be submitted and implemented without approvals, provided that the Severity 1 ticket is attached to RFC"; this has bypassed the approval process and added an additional step in work instruction for attaching a ticket in RFC.

5.1.1 Process vs. Procedure

PROCESS	PROCEDURE
Processes are driven by achievement of a desired outcome.	Procedures are driven by completion of the task.
Process talks about activities and results.	Procedures talk about tasks and deliverables.
Process stages are completed by different people with the same objectives—departments do not matter.	Procedure steps are completed by different people in different departments with different objectives.
Processes flow to conclusions.	Procedures are discontinuous.
Processes focus on fulfilling their purpose.	Procedures focus on satisfying the rules.
Processes transform inputs into outputs through the use of resources.	Procedures define the sequence of steps to execute a task.

Table 5: Process vs procedure

5.1.2 Work Instruction

Work instruction is the smallest and most granular piece of a process that may not be deemed necessary in all cases. In fact, most work instructions are encoded in a tool, and that eliminates the need for a separate document. A user guide in such cases becomes the work instruction. Work instruction is the elements of a procedure, telling the exact steps an individual takes to complete the task and further diminishing the ability to make judgments, which can make procedures bureaucratic. There are several reasons that may still demand a formal work-instruction document:

- Work instruction enhances repeatability.

    This brings consistency and quality to the process. Through continual improvement the work instruction will be changed (under control), until best practice is achieved. Once best practice is achieved, the work instruction will ensure that it is maintained.

- Work instruction facilitates ease of action.

  With a documented process, operators/workers do not have to remember the specifics of the process. They need to know the essentials and where to find the work instruction.

- Work instructions simplify training.

  When new staff are introduced, the work instruction acts as a guideline for delivering a training about how to do a process. A book of work instruction will cover all the processes that need to be taught.

- Work instructions save time.

  Once the initial time has been spent writing the instruction, every time someone refers to the instruction is time saved for management.

Ideally all processes should have work instructions, but it may not be a feasible proposition to create work instruction for obvious things. (The criteria for considering something "obvious" may itself be debatable, like the definition of *common sense* is debatable). I strongly recommend creating work instructions for the process that meets the following criteria:

1. Some variation and deviation is based on the department or group: one common example is a request-fulfillment process. While you are fulfilling a desktop request, the finishing part will differ from that for a laptop. Since the desktops are hardwired to the corporate network internally, you will not include instruction or additional steps to apply for additional security measures that normally would be included for laptops.

2. Some constraints on training are removed (e.g., by remote-location operators). You may like to use work instruction as self-paced training material.

3. Accessible documentation of complex steps that can be difficult to remember is provided. In such cases work instructions will become the most effective tool to eliminate process-run errors.

4. Process has a high impact on business—in such cases you would go the extra mile in taking care and precautions to eliminate errors in run time, and, for this, work instructions become the effective tool.

The level of details included in work instructions is naturally deeper than that of procedures, but the question of how much deeper depends on the following factors:

1. How many reference and supporting documents are available that can be used as cross-reference—if reference documents are available, then you would link them or embed them in the work instruction. This has multiple advantages—not only is the repetitive documentation reduced, but also the accuracy and currency maintenance is easy.

2. Accessibility and quality and comprehension of training material— you may have the deeper and more-detailed documents, but if they are not accessible, then you will be compelled to include details in the work instructions.

3. How complex is the task and how easy to use are the deployed tools— complex tasks will naturally need detailed work instructions, but if the automation is done with tools, then the tool user guide would serve the purpose of work instructions.

4. How often that task is performed—this is a kind of ROI on the effort. Spending time and effort in deeper work instruction will make sense if that task is used frequently.

5. What is the consequence if not done properly—this is important criteria in the context of IT, where people are dealing with crisis all the time.

Publishing standards of work instruction should be consistent with those of process documents.

5.2 Process Models

Basic process model

A basic process model is just good enough to illustrate the basic definition of a process as "a series of tasks connected in logical fashion," as shown in the diagram below.

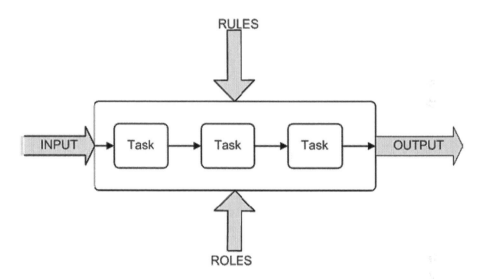

Figure 14: Basic process model

Expanded process model

Now that we understand the basic concept, we need to expand this model for the process-engineering purpose.

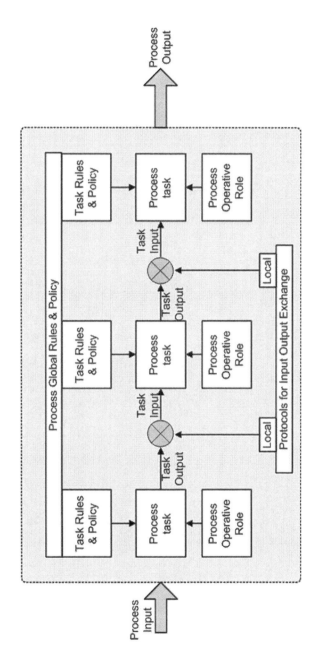

Figure 15: Expanded process model

Input: Something (information, an event, data, etc.) that is fed in for the purpose of transformation into another form or characteristic. *Trigger* is a special kind of event input that initiates the task execution.

Output: Something that is transformed from input by virtue of the task execution. Output of a task feeds to another task as an input. Sometimes the output may not usable as is—there might be a need for protocols for input/ output exchange.

Rule: A prescribed guide for regulating the task execution, this includes policy. There is often a misunderstanding of the difference between policy and rule. While policy is a guideline (non-mandatory) for thinking, a rule is a mandatory prescription. Process rules can be global or confined to selected tasks in the process.

Role: The part played by the task performer is the role. There are usually multiple roles in a process, and process tasks can be distributed across different groups or even different organizations and locations. A role is different than a title or designation.

Incident management is one of the most pervasive processes. Hence it would be beneficial to illustrate this model in the context of an incident-management process.

1. In an incident-management process, "register customer call" is a **task.**

2. A customer call or e-mail is a **trigger**; incident data (issue description, symptom, etc.) are **input.**

3. A ticket number is **output.**

4. "Ticket cannot be created without a valid badge ID" is a **rule.**

5. "Severity value of ticket will be governed by SLA document" is a **policy.**

6. The person who created the ticket in this case performed the **role** of help-desk analyst.

5.2.1 The Functional Process Model

The functional model views the basic model in the context of functions and is used for developing the functional specification for a process. This model is also used for integrating processes.

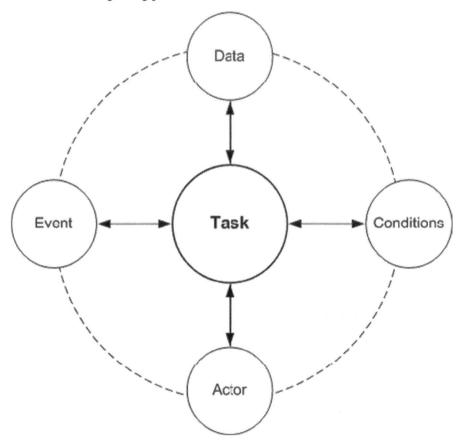

Figure 16: Functional model of a process

This model talks about the four core elements—event, data, actor, and conditions revolving around the task. These elements are connected with tasks with the following functional relationships:

1. The actor is a person or a machine who performs a task. Execution of a task by an actor can notify another actor. In the basic process model, an actor corresponds with a role.

2. An event can begin, end, or halt a task. Also, execution of a task can generate an event. Thus an event can be input or output of a task.

3. A task can produce data. Also, a task may need some data for its execution. Thus data can be input or output of a task.

4. Conditions are a process's environmental state that combines the relationship between event and data with a task. That means a condition can start or end a task or denote some specific data. Conditions do not exactly corresponding to rules of the basic model but rather are a combination of input and output.

5.3 Detailed Process Structure

For the purpose of process management, we will present the management view. In detailed process structure, there will be three blocks: process core, process control, and process enabler.

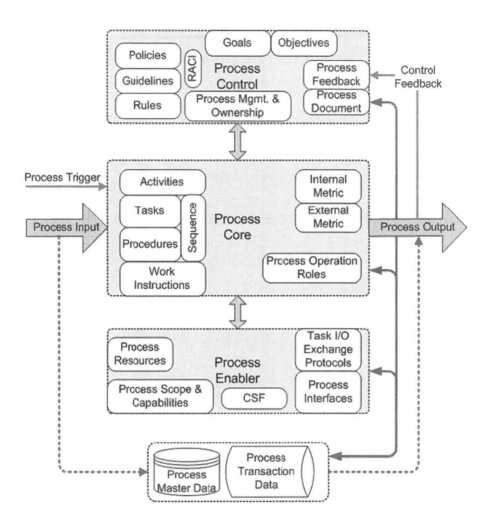

Figure 17: Detailed process structure

5.3.1 Process Core

A process core is the instrumentation of the process that takes the input from the external world and delivers the output. Process inputs can be events and/or data, and the process output can be events and/or data. There is one special kind of input event called a trigger, which indicates the beginning point of the process. A trigger will start the process. A process can have multiple triggers. The process output data could be processed data or unprocessed data. For example, within an incident-management process, incident symptom description is one of the process's inputs; customer detail could be another input. But the trigger would always be a customer call, e-mail, or some system event detected by a monitoring tool. A portion of the output is fed back and is called control feedback, and this feedback will usually be a data or event. For example, within the incident-management process, the output is the resolution, and a notification that is generated to notify the breach of a certain threshold (e.g., group hop count or SLA for resolution) will be the control feedback. Control feedback, either automated or manual, is normally used to correct the performance of the process.

Work-flow

This includes an activity, task, procedure, and work instructions and the relationships among these four elements. All these elements must be connected by a sequence, and it is important to note that a sequence must exist at each level (i.e., activity sequence, task sequence, procedure sequence, and work-instruction sequence). Sequences can be in series or in parallel.

Process metric

For a good process, you will have *internal metrics* as well as *external metrics*. Internal metrics are those KPIs that are related to the internal operation of process. External metrics refer to the KPIs related to the result of process. Take, for example, incident-management process: The key external metric will be response time and resolution time, which will be a direct measurement of the result (i.e., the process is able to deliver the required outcome). External metrics will always be customer-focused. The internal metric for the incident-management process will be the group hop count. You may have some incident tickets that would have met the resolution-time SLA despite bouncing among groups multiple times. The customer may not know how many times his ticket bounced among the groups, and he might be satisfied with the resolution-time SLA. However, for a process manager, this number indicates that the effectiveness of the process is at risk, and assignment policies or procedures may not be working well, or untrained people may be taking the role.

The real purpose of metrics is to help make better decisions. The objective of a metric is to operate as a gauge or indicator of process operation. Metrics aid our making good decisions; they exist to identify gaps in skills or resources required to attain the goal. Good metrics focus on the issues that affect the team and that put attainment of the process goal or objective into jeopardy. Recommended metrics policy meets the following criteria:

- Metrics will be set to measure process performance and not people performance.

- Measurement will be based on system-generated data and not on manually entered data.

- Each process will define it own measurable KPIs.

- Metrics will be based on data points directly collectible by tools.

Process roles

Do not confuse roles with titles or designations of people within the organization. A role is purely a part or character played by an actor in the process. Each role has certain rights and obligations. These rights and obligations are in fact associated with a combination of role and task. It is also important to note that a person can play a multiple role in different processes. In fact, in all organizations, the same people undertake the roles of incident resolver (in incident-management process), change-task implementer (in change-management process) and problem investigator (in problem-management process).

5.3.2 Process Control

Control is the instrument and structure designed to provide reasonable assurance that process objectives will be achieved and that undesired events will be prevented or detected and corrected.

Control objective is a statement of the desired result or purpose to be achieved by implementing control procedures in a particular IT activity. Process control includes

1. policy guidelines and rules,

2. goals and objectives,

3. process management and ownership and RACI (Responsible, Accountable, Consulted and Informed matrix),

4. process document, and

5. process feedback.

Process management is the nucleus of all process controls. The purpose of process control is to

1. measure processes efficiently and effectively,

2. keep processes in line with business objectives,

3. keep processes operating smoothly and reliably,

4. keep processes interacting with each other effectively,

5. process problems and issues identified and resolved,

6. continually improve processes with increased efficiency and effectiveness of recurring activities,

7. ensure ease of process maintenance,

8. demonstrate process effectiveness to auditors and regulators,

9. ensure that processes support the overall IT organization goals and enhance IT value delivery,

10. decrease the number of incidents from policy violations,

11. ensure that policies and associated procedures remain current and effective,

12. optimize process costs,

13. update processes according to business needs, and

14. increase staff awareness of what to do and why.

A process document is the foundation of all process controls, because it establishes the official process as well as the official process owner. The process owner is the most important role outside of the process core. A process owner is not a process operation role. A process owner has complete authority over the process. If an organization wants to have a good process, they must have a named process owner who must be recognized as having full claim, authority, power, and dominion over the process. A process owner is accountable for the result of the process. He or she approves any change in the process and usually should appoint a process manager to manage the process life cycle. Process manager is yet another role outside the process core. A process manager will monitor the process performance using the key internal metric and take appropriate action to meet or improve the process performance. Continual process improvement is also the responsibility of the process manager. Policies, guidelines, and rules are also important controls, because they directly impact the sequences of the task in the process core. Goals and objectives are the target of the process output.

Process RACI

Responsible refers to the person who must ensure that activities are completed successfully. Responsibility is associated with ability and dependability.

Accountable refers to the person or group who has the authority to approve or accept the process (execution of the activities and their result). Accountability refers to answerability for the outcome.

Consulted refers to those people whose opinions are sought on an activity (two-way communication).

Informed refers to those people who are kept up-to-date on the progress of an activity (one-way communication).

5.3.3 Process Enabler

The third block in the process structure is the process enabler, and includes the following components:

1. Process scope and capability
2. Process resources
3. Task I/O exchange protocols and process interface
4. Critical success factor (CSF)

Process scope and capabilities are important design criteria that establish the boundary and functional ability of a process. Process resources define the means and supplies required for the process to work. This includes the people in the operative roles and the tools required to run the process. A process is said to be resource-hungry if it requires many operators and tools to execute the task. In the context of incident management, the scope of a process may be confined to a particular tower in an organization (network, data center, storage, etc.) but it may be capable of managing the incidents of all towers. Not only that, but also it may be capable of handling some functions of the event-management process. Critical success factors are the criteria or prerequisites or elements contributing to the success of the process. Finally, task I/O exchange protocols ensure that each task produces certain output that becomes the input of another task in the sequence. Many times the output may not be directly usable; in such situations, you will require a protocol of exchange. This protocol enables the operation of process across multiple groups, geographies, and organizations. Electronic data exchange is one of the common examples of I/O exchange protocols, and, in multi-vendor IT operations, this becomes very important. The extension of protocol at process level is called process interface. The rights and obligations of task and role that exist in process core and are *internal* to the process become the rights and obligation of process at process interface levels *outside* the boundary of process. For example, the process interface between the incident-management and problem-management process may define the following:

a. Incident management is obligated to deliver the diagnostic analysis data for repetitive incidents.

b. Problem management is obligated to provide the known error database to incident management.

5.3.4 Process Data

Process set-up data

Process set-up data is the non-transactional or configuration data that is required to configure tools or templates. It is similar to the master or reference data used in the application world.

Examples of process set-up data are categorization, field menus, and selection value lists, all of which support organization structure. Badly designed process set-up data is one of the most common reasons for process ineffectiveness. The key weaknesses in process set-up data are caused by poor taxonomy and lack of quality control and consistency in taxonomy. Successful and effective process implementation demands a good understanding of the implications of process set-up data structure and goals.

Badly designed process set-up data is the number one spoiler of process implementation in any tool. A tool will always work with bad data, but process will not be effective. The key weaknesses in process set-up data are caused by

1. poor taxonomy,

2. misuse of categorization data,

3. no taxonomy standards, and

4. no quality control on categorization data.

To ensure successful implementation, it is important to review the data structures and data elements' purpose and to understand the use and implications of each of these data structures and their purpose.

We will consider this point later, in the process design section below.

Process transaction data

The transaction data is produced during the operation of process. All the measurements are done on the transaction data. There are multiple uses for transaction data—mainly measurement of not only service performance and external reporting but also for the internal measurement and primary tool for process management.

What transaction data to collect and track depends on the analysis of processes and the rules that exist to deal with data and events. This is covered in requirements gathering. When analyzing current processes and rules, an analyst must identify the transitional points in the process where data moves from one state to the next. Processes must be designed to handle state transitions—spelling out what is a legal transition and what is illegal.

An analyst will also take into account how various groups of people in the organization will handle the data during stated transitions. When analyzing data tracking needs, a process analyst will identify the following information:

1. The life cycle of the data: data capture, storage, retrieval update, archival, and retirement

2. Types of information that can be tracked together, where data comes from, other processes, and user data entry

3. The potential for redundancy of data entry

4. Where data needs to be just referenced, where consumed, and where reused

5. What kinds of reports and information your users need from your application

Analogy with master data management

All business processes that are automated through some applications have very clear concepts of maser data and transaction data. Master Data Management (MDM) is a vast discipline in the business world (and with much broader scope). Master Data Management is a discipline to maintain enterprise data. It comprises of tools and processes for removing duplicates, standardizing data (Mass Maintaining), incorporating rules to eliminate incorrect data from entering the system in order to create an authoritative source of master data. It is recognized as important discipline of the application-management world. The ITSM world needs to learn a lot from this discipline.

5.3.5 Work-flow vs. Process

Work-flow is a part of process but not the complete process. It is not a component but a subassembly in the structure of process.

Misconception of treating work-flow as process is a common problem in all organizations. Almost all ITSM tools that claim to implement processes are actually offering the work-flow but not the process. Let me offer an illustration of change-management process: The work-flow of a typical change-management process will define RFC submission, assessment, approval, planning, implementation, and closure. Perhaps it will also define work-flow based on certain conditions, such as type A work-flow for emergency change and type B work-flow for nonemergency change. But what is considered as an emergency and what are the criteria for declaring a change as an emergency change and who can do that are the policy questions. If these questions are not answered or made an integral part of the business, the work-flow will fail to deliver the process outcome.

As we shall see later in the book, in chapter 8, in process implementation several policies can be encoded in the tool but not all. Therefore, process operators' judgment will be an important success criterion.

5.4 Process Characteristics

Although we have discussed many characteristics in the detailed process structure, I intend to bring out the following prime characteristics with additional focus:

Process flow

Process flow is the work-flow steps to transform inputs into outputs. It is a set of interconnected work elements (tasks, sub tasks, etc.) that have variety of relationships. The most critical relationship is the relationship and dependencies of these work elements that is how these elements are connected.

Depiction of relationship with precedence diagram:

There are four kinds of precedence relationships:

1. Finish to start: task B can start when task A is finished.

2. Finish to finish: task B is finished as soon as task A is finished.

3. Start to start: start of Task A starts Task B.

4. Start to finish: start of task A finishes task B.

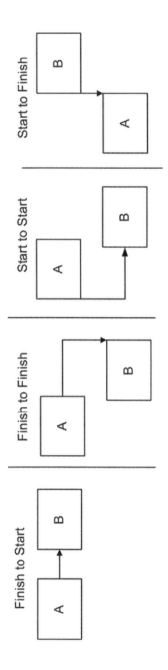

Figure 18: Precedence relationship

Let us understand this little more with a sub process picture

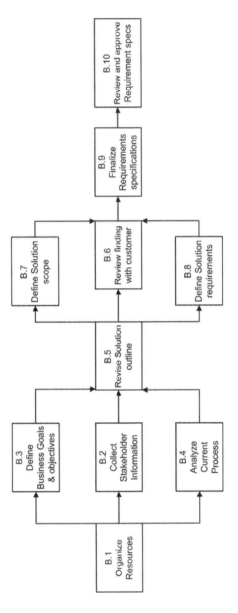

Figure 19: Develop requirements specification precedence diagram

There may be tasks with no predecessors. This would be the case for self-activating tasks when the process has triggers. So task B.1 will have no predecessors.

There may be tasks with no successors either: for example, the last task and sub task of the process for task B.10

Depiction of relationship with Visio diagram:

Visio cross functional diagrams showing the process flow are more popular. I believe the primary reason for this is the popularity of the Visio application and its integration with Microsoft Office. Also, the Visio swim lane provides an easy depiction of the functions to which the tasks are allocated.

In process streamlining we examine these relationships in great detail to set them correctly. Many times these relationships are not enforced in run time and are violated. For example, in an incident-management process, the diagnosis must start only after the incident registration, but a help-desk agent will often ignore the registration of the incident and deliver a resolution on the fly. It is like spending money (giving service) without accounting for it. It also happens often that help-desk agents diagnose and register incidents simultaneously (instead of finish-to-start, they perform the task start-to-start), but then they are not focused on listening to customer symptoms and may take more time to arrive to correctly diagnose the problem, thereby increasing the cycle time and cost of the process.

Process effectiveness

Process effectiveness tells us how well the process output met the customer requirements. Naturally, meeting the final requirements is contingent upon intermediate the output or upon the output of sub processes also meeting the requirements. For example, one of the final outputs of an incident-management process is the resolution. So the process will meet one of the effectiveness criteria if the resolution really fixed the issue. In order to deliver the right resolution, the diagnosis ought to be correct, and for that to happen, symptoms must be recorded corrected. The very first sub process of incident management is registering an incident, and the symptom description is one of the data input generated at the source of the process. This sub process must be effective for the final output.

The customer is the primary beneficiary of process effectiveness. Effectiveness of process can always be improved, regardless of how effective it is currently. This is one of the continual improvement responsibilities that are undertaken by process-management functions.

Process efficiency

Process efficiency tells us how well resources are used to produce an output. The service provider is the primary beneficiary of the process efficiency, and the customer is the secondary beneficiary. Continual process improvement also looks at efficiency improvement. One of the common methods to improve efficiency is to automate routine tasks. Most mistakes are made here. Of course, inefficiency is a problem, but wrong automation is much larger problem.

Another method to improve efficiency is to eliminate tasks that do not add value. This also requires careful consideration, because there are several tasks that are required for internal value, though they may not mean anything to the customer. For example, maintenance activities to keep the services in running condition or security software installation (if the customer has not asked for security) before delivering a laptop add values internally and are necessary to deliver the service that the customer has asked for, though the customer has not asked for these specific tasks.

Process cycle time

Process cycle time tells us the time taken to transform input to final output. There is a difference between cycle time and processing time. A service request to install software may go through the several steps, such as license accounting, approval, and installation. Each step of actual license update or approval or installation may take five minutes, but the complete fulfillment of the service will happen in a few days, not in fifteen minutes.

Cycle time reduction is very specific to every process, and, in transaction-based processes, queue management is one of the prime techniques to optimize the cycle time.

Process cost

Cost tells us the expense of an entire process. There are various cost models to calculate the cost; because the ITSM industry is not yet reached that maturity level, I shall defer my opinion on cost models.

5.5 Explanation of Process Roles

5.5.1 Process Owner

The process owner is the person who *owns the process* as an *asset*. The ownership is tied with the accountability for the result that is expected from the process. This means that the process owner owns all the components of the process—he or she signs off the process document and policies. If a process needs to be changed, the process owner must approve that change. He or she is accountable to keep the process aligned with business needs. The process owner usually appoints a process manager to monitor and maintain the process.

In all IT organizations, we do have asset owners such as server owners, application owners, and others, but rarely do organizations understand the importance of process ownership. Process ownership is very critical to the quality of a process itself and therefore to the quality of the service it is producing. The right candidate for this job will be a person who not only is directly impacted by a bad process but also has the following:

1. Resources to spare

2. Serious interest

3. Sufficient time to spare

4. Adequate influence, power, and authority in the organization

5. Leadership skills

6. Process knowledge

Naturally, we are talking about a senior person in the organization; such a person would not be able to allocate adequate time for several process-management tasks. Therefore, the process owner would outsource these activities to another role: process manager. Please note the word *outsource* is used here, not *delegate*. The intent is the same, but outsourcing implies that an external service provider might take up this job. In a typical outsourcing situation, the outsourcing provider will use and operate the process and optionally also manage on behalf of the process owner.

5.5.2 Process Manager

A process manager is the administrator of the process who monitors and maintains the performance of the process. The *process manager* is *responsible* for the *functionality* of the process, while the *process owner* is *accountable* for the *result* of the process.

The process manager does not execute the process tasks but audits the tasks' execution, policy, and compliance. He or she also measures the internal KPIs of the process to determine the health condition of the process. Continual process improvement is the extended responsibility of the process manager. When determining an improvement opportunity that requires policy or work-flow change, a process manager obtains the approval of process manager to implement it.

5.5.3 Process Operator

A process operator executes process tasks assign to his or her role. As a role-player, the process operator is responsible for the task but not accountable for the result of process. He is accountable for the standards and quality of the task deliverable but not the process result.

Process operators exist in multiple roles, as outlined in the table below:

Common Operator Role in Incident-Management Process	Common Operator Role in Problem-Management Process	Common Operator Role in Change-Management Process
incident reporter	problem reporter	change requestor
incident manager/critical incident manager	problem investigator	change implementer
incident resolvers		change approver

Table 6: process operation roles

5.6 Process-Management Roles vs. Process-Operation Roles

As you see in the detailed process structure diagram 17, the process-management role falls in the control block of the process structure, while the process operation roles fall in the core block of the process structure. Prevailing naming conventions of process roles are not adequate to differentiate this fundamental difference. In order to clarify, I offer an example of specific roles—incident manager (IM) and incident management process manager (IMPM)—that I define as an operation role and a management role, respectively.

Consider a typical situation of handling pending tickets in operation. A ticket is pending for a reason: "inputs/missing information required from customer." The incident manager in this situation will review the ticket, identify the reason why the information from the customer is pending, and remove the barrier with appropriate actions—in this case, follow up with the customer, obtain the required information, and move the ticket forward.

The IMPM will not work on transactions but on the process itself. In this case, he or she will review the reason information from the customer is pending and realize that the adequate information is not being collected by the process or invalid information is being collected. He or she will subsequently introduce a rule at the beginning point to enforce or validate the input data (or find some method to automate the missing information collection). This is an act of process improvement or efficiency enhancements.

Incident Manager	Incident-Management Process Manager
Works on transaction (tickets) life cycle	Works on process life cycle
Manages the transaction	Manages the process
Deals with the existing tickets	Makes provisions to deal with future tickets
Monitors the progress of tickets	Monitors the performance of process
The goal is to achieve SLAs.	The goal is to achieve process effectiveness and efficiency.
Services end customers	Services "internal" customers (incident resolvers and IMs)
The approach is incident-oriented—it resolves the incidents that block the operational progress of a process.	The approach is problem-oriented— it eliminates the root cause of an operational problem of a process.

Table 7: Incident manager vs Incident management process manager

Illustration

In an organization, the reopened ticket counts were exceeding the acceptable limit. The IM would review the reopened case and find that the main reason for reopening was that the resolution did not work. Further, the IM also checked the validity and concluded that the resolutions were indeed not correct, while the resolver believed they were correct. The IM handled each reopened ticket by calling the customer and promising her the right service in the next attempt (trying to win a good customer satisfaction rating!) and followed up with the resolver. This is all about managing the operational incident. The IM also asked for help from the IMPM to find out the problem.

The IMPM saw an opportunity to fix the problem. She observed that the reopening was particularly high for the tickets reported by phone and passed on to the second level but not for the tickets opened on the web or by e-mail. Then she noticed that the resolutions were also seemingly correct for the issue/symptom reported. She also observed that the resolution that eventually worked was not relating to the original symptom. This indicated that the symptom recorded in the ticket was not the exact issue that the customer spelled out. The symptom reported by a customer is one of the most significant pieces of information, because this sets the direction and approach of analysis and debugging. A wrong symptom was leading the resolver in the wrong direction to arrive at the wrong destination.

What was the problem in noting the correct symptom and recording in the ticket? Why was the reopening rate so much higher for phone-reported issues? The answer is "distorted symptom." A further cause of this distortion is *habit*. Service-desk agents are highly conditioned by frequently reported issues. They would not listen carefully but hear what they want to hear. This would record an ambiguous/incorrect/incomplete symptom and set the weak foundation for investigation and diagnostic. On an e-mail or web ticket there would not be any distortion of information.

The IMPM modified the process and added one step in registering the incident: "read back the symptom description to the customer and verify that it is correctly recorded." This two-minute addition in the time to create a ticket prevented many possible reopens and increased customer satisfaction.

One of the biggest challenges in implementing and adopting process-management function in an organization is the lack of concepts behind the idea. In almost every case where I have come across process managers, I found that they were in mixed-up roles—the operation role and management role were mixed up. Typical process management responsibilities should include the following:

- Support on process
- Training
- FAQ support
- Correct broken process
- Proactive improvement
  - Monitor process performance through internal KPIs
  - Identify process bottlenecks and improvement opportunities
  - Initiate and complete improvement projects
- Process-configuration maintenance and template maintenance
  - Baseline the tool configuration for the process
  - Maintain the process set-up data for the respective processes
  - Maintain the integrity of process configuration data
  - Maintain process documents

5.6.1 Process—the Instrument to Control Entropy

In our college physics, we learned about entropy—under the law of thermodynamics. In thermodynamics, entropy is the property that determines the energy available for useful work. I would take this concept of physics and apply it to the service-management domain of IT organizations. So entropy determines the resources available for *useful* work.

In plain English, *entropy* is defined as the degree of disorder or uncertainty in the system. Typical attributes are chaos, disorganization, and randomness.

The second law of thermodynamics says that the entropy of a system will increase relentlessly if you do not do anything to control it. If we apply this analogy to IT, it means that service performance, system performance, and so on will degrade automatically within a period of time if we do not take appropriate steps to maintain it. As we saw in section 2.2.1, service production is the combination of technology-independent ITSM process and technology- and product-specific technical process. These are the two prime controls to manage the entropy of IT and therefore the service derived from IT.

Entropy can be created internally as well as externally. The external entropy is caused by the incompatibility among product vendors and technology that we often see in almost all IT organizations. While each vendor provides the best practice to manage the individual technology, the cross-vendor integration is often inadequate and automatically increases the entropy of the organization.

Internal entropy is created by people working with disintegrated processes and focusing on wrong issues. In order to eliminate the negative impact of entropy, we need both technical- and service-process management. In other words, a well-designed process will begin with a minimum baseline entropy value and thus establish a system of order in managing the service. However, if you let the process remain static, and you do nothing to make that process dynamically change with the service need, entropy will increase relentlessly. Therefore, process management becomes an imperative need.

While process is a powerful instrument to control entropy, it is still not an easy solution to adopt to become a process-driven organization. Implementation of process will not reduce the effort or hard work necessary. It will only shift the focus from crisis management to planning. In other words, without managed process you will be doing hard work in dealing with crisis, but with managed process you will be busy in planning and avoiding crisis. It is like making efforts to remain healthy. You need to take out time to do daily workouts, be strongly disciplined in your diet, and follow healthy protocols. There is lot of difference between staying healthy and staying alive. Similarly, there is lot of difference between IT that is running and IT that is robust.

5.6.2 Process Does Not Eliminate Analytical Thinking

While process has great deal to do with producing good service, it does not eliminate the need and importance of analytical thinking. In fact, process provides a platform, foundation, methodology, and direction for analysis, but true analysis is still done with brains. For example, there may be a problem-management process in place, but that by itself does not actually solve problems.

You use a method and the analytical thinking to solve a problem. Process provides the method and data but cannot provide *thinking*.

6 DESIGNING/REENGINEER A PROCESS

Considerations for a robust process design are suggested in the diagram 18 below. A process is considered as robust by virtue of the following characteristics:

Resiliency—this refers to design that will bring the progression of the process to the right track, even if it is drifted from the original path. For example, a customer's providing a wrong symptom diverted the resolution responsibility to a different technical area (from operating system symptoms to the database symptom), but, at the first available opportunity, the correct assignment path was set because of checks and balances.

Durability and maintainability—durability refers to how enduring is the process in the time frame of business. Durability is also created by maintenance, and that is where maintainability becomes very important. How easily it can be updated with business needs! There are certain techniques for adding insignificant activity steps for future expansion. For example, I add one step for "WIP" after "Assigned" in the life cycle of a ticket. This additional step will allow creating an additional time stamp, and therefore OLA measurement that may not be required today. Or, in a multi-vendor situation, the same step can be used to measure Vendor 1 and Vendor 2 interfaces.

Ability to withstand abuse—one common example is sending the ticket in a pending state to dodge the SLA. Adequate process design will prevent such abuses.

Ability to enforce compliance—certain checks and balances will allow compliance enforcement.

Robustness of a process comes in degrees; the more of these attributes that are present, the more robust a process is. A process may be very robust, but you may still face operational problems. However, those causes will be external. Let me draw an analogy with highways: A town planner designs highways to take people from start to end point in a journey. The goals are to take people as fast as possible but safely. While all safety factors and speed-enabling factors are accounted, and the highway is constructed, accidents still happen, and traffic still slows down even without accidents. These are external factors—you have encounter unskilled drivers who may cause accidents or clueless drivers figuring out directions and exits, thereby slowing down traffic.

You will encounter a similar situation in process operations. Untrained and unskilled process operators may slow down or create an illusion of process breakdown.

The following diagram illustrates a typical design approach for a process.

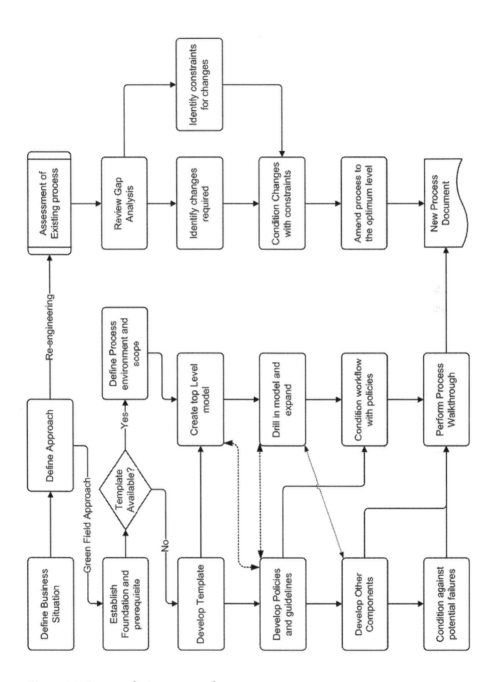

Figure 20: Process design approach

6.1 Greenfield Approach vs. Reengineering Approach

The term greenfield was originally used in construction and development to reference land that has never been used (e.g. green or new), where there was no need to demolish or rebuild any existing structures. Today, the term greenfield project is used in many industries, including software development where it means to start a project without the need to consider any prior work. The greenfield approach implies a radical turnaround. A greenfield approach is applied to the design and formation of a new process and working practices. A greenfield approach asks the following question: "If a new organization is formed, what process would it adopt?" In this approach you disregard the existing process and start on a clean slate. You may still choose to see the existing process components (such as policy or metric) but without any compulsion to inherit. A greenfield approach gives an opportunity to design from a fresh look, and it still brings in the mature process. The disadvantage of this approach is the requirement for extensive training and well-planned organization change management. To avoid these disadvantages, this approach is usually adopted when there is radical change in the organization by virtue of outsourcing. This approach is also useful when there is change in the underlying tool set that automates the process.

A process reengineering approach does not radically change the existing process but improves upon it by tweaking and tuning its components. Process improvement principles apply in this approach. While improvement refers to limited tweaking and amendments, reengineering involves extensive changes. The advantage is that the adoption of a reengineered process is easier than the adoption of a new process altogether. The disadvantage is that you may still live with some legacy that you otherwise would like to quit. Reengineering always starts with the assessment of existing processes.

6.1.1 Do Not Fix Unbroken Things

One of the common mistakes during process design, especially with a reengineering approach, is the tendency to fix the things that are not broken. I have seen this in many areas—for example, ITIL V3 attempted to fix several things of ITIL V2 that were not broken. And what they want to simplify (configuration management and CMDB guidance) in ITIL v2, they made it more complicated in ITIL V3 by making it configuration management system (CMS) and service asset and configuration management (SACM.) There is not a clear distinction between an asset and a CI in ITIL v2 (I explain this later in section 5.14); however, instead of addressing that lack of clarity, it brought up the more-complicated concept of CMS and SACM. If the industry has been struggling to implement the core concept of CMDB and configuration management, then why complicate it further? If something is working well, there is no need to change it. The change here is not with respect to the improvement. You should always make existing things better but only *after* you have fixed the broken things. The first priority is always to make the process effective, and making it efficient is the second priority.

In the software world, there is a lot of temptation to release the next version of software that will fix the things that are not broken. In this book, later, in section 8.5 I briefly discuss the tool trap, in which the new version of a tool comes, and that is claimed as the process improvement. It is like replacing one broken thing with another broken thing.

6.1.2 Righteous Thing vs. Popular Thing

Often there is a conflict between righteousness and populism. Right things may not be popular. A process-led approach will lead to enforcement of discipline. It is a matter of writing a balanced diet for the health of IT service. You do not eat junk food all the time, but you do not eat boiled vegetables all the time either. You cannot sustain the bad practice in long run, and you will be forced to adopt the right things at some point of time, so why not sooner rather than later? People understand that the rule of law is good to avoid the chaos, but that understanding may not be strong enough to adopt discipline. As I said earlier, there are much larger benefits in staying healthy than just being alive and dragging on.

You may find some part of the organizations keen to adopt good practice and undertake disciplines more than others. For example, in one organization, we implemented a change-management process and linked it to configuration management and configuration management database (CMDB.) I signed one policy statement from all stakeholders, and that said, "Each RFC must be related to at least one configuration item." This rule was enforced in the system. Before this enforcement, all use cases were explored—like what if RFC is needed on a CI, and that CI is not available in CMDB—and for each of the use cases, recourse was also established; for example, in this case a generic CI was created. (Use of generic configuration item CI will also give the measurement of CMDB maturity and the maturity of configuration-management process. If too many RFCs are related to a generic CI, that means either CMDB is not complete or people are taking the shortcuts). When this rule went in production, there was a lot of push back from a few support groups. I saw a clear polarization—many groups against it, some neutral, and very few supporting it. Eventually the system enforcement of this rule was withdrawn. What happened after that? The manager of database groups enforced this rule upon his team members, and he will not approve any change unless the RFC is related to database CI. (He was in an approval chain for all database changes.) His team did not like it, but this allowed him to trace incidents on database and relate them to RFC. Over a period of time, the change-management system has enough data to report what kind of changes could produce what kind of incident and how to avoid the risks.

In short, the decision-makers in the organization need to make the choice when to become popular and when to become right. They might have opportunity to be right and popular both, but that kind of opportunity may not exist all the time.

6.2   Establish a Foundation

There are certain things that are prerequisite or a foundation to build a robust process.

The goal is identified.

An early step in creating a robust process is to establish its overall objective, document it, share it with all stakeholders, and ensure that all process-design participants agree to it and clearly understand it. The objective should answer the questions of what problem the process solves, which issues it addresses, and how the process adds value and quality to the environment.

The executive sponsor is identified and involved.

Each process needs to have an executive sponsor who is seriously interested in the successful design and ongoing execution of the process. This person provides support, resources, insight, and executive leadership. The executive sponsor uses his or her clout for any required participation or communication with diversified groups, either inside or outside the organization. This individual is often a level up in the organizational hierarchy from the process owner.

The process owner is identified.

The process owner should not only be identified but also given responsibility and authority over the process. This person leads the team that designs the process, identifies its key customers and suppliers, and documents its use. The process owner executes, communicates, and measures the effectiveness of the process on an ongoing basis.

Key customers are identified and involved.

Key customers are those individuals who are the immediate users and direct beneficiaries of the process. For example, suppose you're designing processes to fulfill requests of IT users. Key customers for this would be users who are most likely to request these services on a regular basis. The IT service desk is deemed to represent all the users who would be one of the key customers, and of course all fulfilling groups, including the service desk, who act and use this process would be key customers as well. Their involvement in developing the process is important to ensure practical design and ease of use.

6.3 Engineering Principles

Develop around outcome, not tasks.

Tasks are an important part of the process, but tasks do not dictate the outcome of the process. It is always other way round—the desired outcome will dictate what tasks need to be built. Take an example of change-management process: Most cases I witness are focusing on completion of a change within the approved time duration. However, the desired outcome is to have a *successful* implementation of change. And change would be deemed successful when the change advisory board (CAB) has agreed that the transaction has achieved the purpose, but that is not good enough. Considering the completion of a transaction as the goal of the process is a common mistake. We should also ensure that the process has also achieved its goal. That means, for the first part, there ought to be a post-implementation review, and there ought to be some success criteria. For the second part, the goal of change management is also to maintain the integrity of the production environment and act as a prime control for configuration management. That means the CMDB should be updated on completion of change.

Take another example of availability management process: The desired outcome from an availability-management process is a sustained level of availability at agreed cost. This is not a transaction-based process. This is among the most misunderstood processes. If we organize around this outcome, we will realize that this process as a whole becomes a vantage-point process with the following criteria:

1. What should be the cost of required (sustained) availability is established by service-level management (SLM) process. Establishing

availability requirements and concluding availability SLA is really an activity outside the availability-management process but should be organized within availability-management process as vantage point.

2. Activities related to availability monitoring and take-control actions on events impacting availability is in the scope of an event- and incident-management process.

3. Measuring and reporting and initiating availability improvements are scoped under SLM and CSI processes.

4. An incident-and-problems-management process deals with the incidents and problems that impact availability.

5. IT processes such as change management and backup and recovery Management have a direct impact on availability, while other processes, such as managing configuration changes, may have only an indirect impact.

Availability management should be organized as a specific set of interrelated IT processes and tools that need to be viewed and managed from a single vantage point in order to achieve the desired outcome.

Goals need to be driving factors.

What output is considered as achievement of goal? For example, if you consider that the goal of incident management is to deliver the resolution, then the process will end as soon as the resolution is delivered. However, as we have seen in real life, it is not only important to deliver the resolution, but also what counts is the right resolution: that means there should be an explicit confirmation from the customer that the resolution served the intended purpose.

While goals are the driving factors that are directly linked to the process, there are objectives also, which are linked to the sub process and purpose (which in turn are linked to the task). If you achieve the purpose of task, you will achieve the objective of resources and therefore the goal of the process. For your ready reference, the goals and objectives of some of the processes are listed below.

Process	Goal	Objectives
Incident management	To restore normal service as quickly as possible	Incidents are not lost, and every incident is recorded. (Incident detecting and recording sub process) Life cycle of each incident is monitored and progress is tracked. (incident monitoring sub process)
Problem management	Identify and eliminate the root of problems and improve the service quality.	Adequate support and help is rendered to incident management to resolve incidents quickly. (known error database (KEDB) maintenance and work-around validation)
Change management	Maintain the integrity of production environment.	Each change is recorded and assessed. (RFC submission and review) Changes do not conflict with each other. (FSC) Each RFC is approved. (approval process)

Process	Goal	Objectives
Availability management	Optimize the capability of IT infrastructure services and supporting organization to deliver sustained level of service.	Ensure IT services are designed to deliver the required level of availability. Reduce unavailability through a well-designed and -executed availability plan.
Capacity management	All current and future capacity and performance aspects of business requirements are provided cost-effectively.	Components are used optimally (performance monitoring and tuning) Monitor analyze and report on service performance (service capacity management)

Table 8: Process goals and objectives

Increase the stakes of process "internal" beneficiary.

If possible, have those who *use* the output of process, *perform* the process task. This will help ensure that people will produce the right output. Take, for example, a task of registering an incident: The purpose of this task is to create a unique incident ID for tracking purposes throughout the life cycle. Incident ID is generated by the system when input data is fed. One of the input data is the symptom description. I have seen very often that the symptom description is not recorded properly and adequately, and it impacts the diagnosis at the next level. If a person who is collecting this data is also responsible to use this data for resolution purposes, there will be a natural tendency to collect the right data for investigation and diagnosis. There are two possible situations here:

a. If the job of the help desk is to register and dispatch the incident, then the help-desk agent's tendency will be to collect only the data that is good enough to determine the group to whom the ticket needs to be dispatched.

It is quite possible that after assignment the resolution group discovers that the data is not sufficient to carry out investigation and diagnosis.

b. If the job of the help-desk agent is to register the incident and also make an attempt to resolve at the first level (that is, they have first call resolution rate (FCR) SLA) in that case, there will be assurance that adequate symptoms description is recorded, which will help them to perform initial diagnostic action.

Similarly, it is more likely that the change request will have complete information if the requestor has adequate participation in implementation as well.

Incorporate data collection work as an integral part of actual work.

Data collection is extremely important work during the run time of the process, while the real work in any process is the work that produces an intermediate output, end output, or a component of the end output. So if investigation and diagnosis is a task in an incident-management process, then filling in diagnostic data must be a part of the diagnosis task.

For time measurements, rely on system-generated data.

I strongly recommend that you let the system automatically produce the data that it can produce by itself, and that you use system-generated information as far as possible. I came across one customer-specific requirement about the measurement of SLA/OLA in an incident-management process. The customer wanted to measure the response time as well as resolution time of a field technician. This customer implemented a system whereby a date/time field was created in the ticket and introduced the procedure that the field technician was expected to use to enter this data for all the tickets assigned to him or her. Value in this field was used to calculate the response-time SLA. Guess what? Every field technician achieved the SLA consistently. In reality the field technicians knew what time they need to enter to achieve the SLA, and indeed they will enter the time to achieve the SLA. In other words, producing additional information of the date/time of arrival at the user desk has no value.

Treat geographically dispersed resources as though they were centralized.

Do not break a process task based on geography. With the pervasive network and process running in a tool that is accessible across the world, it is no longer necessary to design tasks for specific geography or location. Do not confuse geography with the policies that usually differ in each location. People residing in any location can work remotely but as they are geographically or physically present.

Link parallel activities instead of integrating their results.

When an incident is detected, the process aims to resolve it as quickly as possible, and it can be resolved using a work-around, while problem management does not work under the same time pressure but instead identifies the root. In some cases, incident management and problem management run in parallel. While incident management is seeking a work-around, problem management is seeking the root of the incident. The common share is the development of work-around, and both process activities can be linked where incident management develops the work-around, and problem management validates the work-around.

Monitoring the progress is always a parallel activity and linked across all the tasks of the process.

Put the decision points where the work is performed.

While building tasks, do not assume that only specialists can perform complex work. The fact is that the knowledge-base systems and experts systems enable task actors adequately to perform the standard or routine work as good as it need be.

Similarly, while building the controls, do not assume that managerial hierarchy is required for control and supervision. The fact is that the accessible data, analytical tool, and exception monitoring eliminate the need for direct supervisory control.

Decision about the risk is one of the control attributes of RFC.

Capture information once and at the source.

When the event of a potential problem is detected by an event-management process, it collects the basic data of a configuration item (CI) behavior. This data is used for control response on events. The same data could be used by an incident-management process (if the event eventually became an incident) and, further, by problem management as well, if required.

Do not fix the things that are not broken.

(As explained in section 5.1.1.)

6.4   *Define the Process Environment, Scope, and Boundary*

It is very important to understand and document the environment in which the process will work. IT organization may be fragmented into different units based on a variety of criteria such as geography, business units, and the internal IT organization itself. A very common scenario is differentiation of infrastructure and application. You may design a patch-management process or change-management process that will that will run only within infrastructure environment and not for applications. Here are the key questions to ask:

Where does the process start? Does my incident-management process start with the detection of an event that is likely to degrade the service (but service is still running OK at this moment), *or* does it start when the service is really impacted?

Another situation: a user has reported an incident by an e-mail. This e-mail is sitting in the mailbox of the service-desk queue. Has the incident-management process started?

Where does the process end? Does my change-management process end upon the completion of the change implementation, or does it end a few weeks later, when the change has been deemed to be a successful implementation?

Another situation: Does my request fulfillment process end when I deliver the required laptop to the user, or does it end when it has joined the domain after delivery—or even when, after joining the domain, the profile from an old laptop has been migrated to new laptop?

Where are the inputs entered? Are all intermediate inputs generated within the process, or do they also come from an external process? I have triggered my patch-management process by an input—e-mail from Microsoft—on the second Tuesday of the month. Where and when will the actual patch be inputted in the process? Where will current configuration data enter in process?

What are the points of output? Is the final output the only output? What about intermediate output? Are intermediate outputs required only for internal consumption, or are they also needed for external consumption?

What is included in the process? And what is not included—not only from the perspective of deliverables but also within the overall scope? For example, does a service-request-management process include catalog maintenance?

Another example: through the problem-management process, we have found the root cause of the defect/bug reported via incident. Now the coding (development work actually in CMM life cycle) for testing and deployment—should it go to change-and-release management? Many times the solution development and testing happen within problem management.

Who are the actors involved? If there are activities, there will be actors. Each actor has some role name in the process, but there could be some actors outside the role who still influence and impact the process operation. Do you formalize those in a process? For example, in a problem-management process, if the problem investigation may be carried out by an investigator role, but in proactive reality there will be more than one person investigating, who will update the ticket with the investigation work log?

6.5   Develop a Template

The content of process documentation should be considered complete if it includes the following:

1.   Goals and objectives of the process (vision and mission)

2.   Service delivery and support environment; scope (boundary)

3.   Policies and guidelines

4.   Inputs and outputs, triggers, communication

5.   Process flow diagram

6.   Process activities description/explanation in details

7.   Interface with other processes

8.   Associated documentation

9.   Role names and responsibilities, owner, users

10. CSF dependencies and KPIs

11. Measurement and reporting

At the end of the design, the outcome is a process on paper that should clarify these topics. A process document should support and assure that the process is described by a sound business model that makes common business sense. The benefits of using the process should exceed the cost and efforts of a complete process-management life cycle—design, implementation, and run.

Process hierarchy in the document must be clearly understood. Every process will have sub processes underneath it. They will also have relationships with other service-management processes. Individuals who are developing well-designed, robust processes know and understand the relationships between processes.

It is important to make sure that execution is enforceable in operations. Many policies in the process need to be enforceable to be effective. With easily available technology today, it is possible and practical to encode policy in the enabling tools and enforce policy during run time, including through authorizations, audit trails, or locks. When technical enforcement is not practical, management support, review boards, metrics, or other procedural techniques should ensure enforcement.

The process must be designed to provide service metrics as well as process metrics (that is, internal as well as external measurements). Most processes measure something associated with their output. Often this involves a quantitative measure, such as transaction processes per second or jobs completed per hour. In addition, a robust process focuses on qualitative measures that are oriented toward the end user. These metrics show the relative quality of the service being provided.

Documentation must be thorough, accurate, and easily understood. Documentation is one of the fundamentals that clearly separate mediocre infrastructures from those that are truly world-class. Well-written documentation facilitates the training, maintenance, and marketing of key processes. Thorough documentation eases the tasks of removing all non–value-added steps and verifying that all required value-added steps are present.

The process must contain all required value-added steps. The process should also eliminate all non–value-added steps. If a step is not directly contributing value to the overall objective of the process, process designers should eliminate that step.

The process needs to guarantee accountability. Analysts should use process metrics, performance charts, and trending reports to quickly identify when a department or an individual is not following the prescribed procedure, with direct feedback to and consequences from management. For this design to work, process designers and owners need to give management sufficient tools to carry out enforcement. In turn, management needs to follow up with fair, timely, and appropriate actions to ensure process compliance in the future. The process should provide incentives for compliance and penalties for avoidance or circumvention.

The process must be standardized across all towers and remote sites. Designers may develop some processes at different remote sites and at different times. Nonstandard processes often come into play as a result of acquisitions, mergers, or takeovers. The technical challenge of implementing an agreed-upon standard is often much easier than the political challenge of actually reaching that consensus in the first place.

The process needs to be automated wherever practical, but only after streamlining. Automation can end up being either beneficial or detrimental, depending on how the automation is designed and implemented. Automation of a poorly designed manual process results in doing a bad job more quickly and with less effort.

The process needs to integrate with all other appropriate processes. Several processes within systems management naturally complement each other. For example, problem and change management are separate processes, but they often rely on each other for optimum effectiveness. Similarly, performance tuning and capacity planning are almost always closely related.

6.6   Create a Top-Level Model

A top-level model is the list of sub processes or high level activities that you will do under that process. This would be the happy path from start to finish, with no conditions attached. This is foundation on which you will build the process. To clarify, here are a few top-level models:

Change management

1. RFC initiation

2. Initial review and prioritization

3. Assessment and approval

4. Planning and implementation

5. Post implementation review and closure

Availability management

1. Availability risk assessment and management

2. Implement cost-justifiable countermeasures

3. Monitor, measure, review, and analyze availability reports for components and service

4. Investigate service and component unavailability and instigate remedial measures

Capacity management

1. Capacity management framework

2. Capacity plan

3. Capacity database

4. Modeling

5. Tuning

6. Application sizing

7. Demand management

IT service continuity management

1. Identify business service continuity requirements

2. Create and maintain IT service continuity strategy and plan

3. Prepare IT service-continuity capability

4. Review and test IT service-continuity plan

6.6.1 Identify the Roles at Top-Level Models

For each sub process or top-level activity, identify who will do that activity. It could be one or more roles for each activity. Map the roles—you may have more than one role in one sub process. After mapping, create a swim-lane model.

6.7 Drill in Model and Expand

Now you can start developing the sections' content in logical sequence according to your thinking rhythm. The logical sequence refers to what can be written in parallel and what can be written in series. For example, you cannot define "trigger" unless you define and determine "inputs" of the process. Thus I/O section should be defined before your work-flow. Similarly, you cannot define roles and responsibilities, unless you have defined activities. However, while you are defining work-flow, you can simultaneously develop policies and guidelines. Your thinking rhythm may lead you to switch back and forth between the sections, and you should not try to curtail your thinking. You may even add inconsistent things in different sections of the process, but do not worry during the development stage. It is a kind of assembly of individual sections and then fitting them together. While you are doing final assembly, you can trim the parts correctly to fit with each other.

In the first go, you will have the top-level work-flow at the sub-processes' level and drill down each sub process separately to the task level.

6.8 Develop Policies and Guidelines

When you started with the top-level model, you will be able to list process-level policies and guidelines. As you ponder on tasks, ask several questions, such as the ones that follow:

1. What if the wrong inputs or invalid inputs are received?

2. What if prerequisites are not available?

3. How can this task be done?

4. How should it be done?

5. Why should it be done that way?

6. What if I do not do it the way it should be done?

7. What are the different scenarios under which the task will be performed (use cases)?

Try to play devil's advocate in task performance, and you will have clues about the right policies. Take, for example, the series of tasks that are normally performed when you receive a call and register an incident at the help desk. What if the customer provides the wrong ID, and you cannot locate customer in database? Or what if the customer is asking for a service that is not in your scope? What if a customer demands higher priority?

Following are a few examples in an incident-management process that will add some decision boxes in the work-flow when you apply these policies:

- Cancellation policy

- Ticket-closing policy

- Prioritization policy

- Dispute on prioritizing

- Priority-change policy

- Keeping tickets in pending state

- Dispute on scope

- Policy for reopened tickets

6.9 Develop Other Components

6.9.1 Determine Roles

Process actors or operation roles are very critical and must be clearly specified. The naming convention should be consistent across all processes. Each role will have at least one of the four types of association in RACI: namely, responsibility, accountability, consulted, and informed.

Roles vs. title vs. job description

A role is the name of the part that a person plays in the process operation. A title is the designation in the HR system or in the organization. A job description details the things that person is supposed to do and is usually well beyond the process roles. So a person with title senior system engineer can take the role of problem investigator in a problem-management process and of a change implementer in a change-management process, and that job description will include not only system management but also might include people management.

Multitasking vs. multiple roles

Throughout the organization, process roles are invariable shared. The same person can play a role in incident management, problem management, change management, availability management, capacity management, and so on.

Multitasking is entirely different than playing multiple roles. A person can multitask in the same role or across multiple roles. People wrongly believe that multitasking is critical in IT service delivery and support.

This belief is based on the assumption that human beings are capable of doing two cognitive tasks at the same time. That is absolutely wrong. What really happens is that a person learns to move rapidly between tasks. For example, you are attending a conference call and "simultaneously" checking e-mail—at this moment you're missing what's happening on the call for the duration of your act of checking your e-mail. Also, you're spending a finite amount of "switching time," the time it takes to shift from one cognitive activity to another.

Switching time increases the amount of time it takes to finish the primary task you were working on, and therefore multitasking is incredibly inefficient. (Computers' CPU cycle time, analogous to switching time, is measured in nanoseconds, so computers can multitask, but that speed and efficiency is not possible for humans.)

6.9.2 Establish Measurements and KPI

We know a general rule of business—if you cannot measure, then you cannot manage. We need a variety of measurements to understand what is occurring, what bottlenecks are, what are the needs for change, what targets should be set, and where improvement can be made. A major problem in almost all process measurements is that the performance is measured only for the end outcomes, and those are external SLAs. The right measurement system would measure not only the quality of outcome but also the health parameter of the processes itself (we called this the "internal" measurement in an earlier section (4.3.1). The assumption that if the end product is OK, then the process is OK is not correct all the time. The end product may be OK, but it may be consuming more resources than should be necessary to produce it, or someone may be correcting it outside the process.

You should establish the measurement system based on the answer to two key concerns—what needs to be measured and why it needs to be measured. It is important to understand that not everything can or should not be measured.

I hear that the major barrier to invest in process management is the difficulty in measuring return on investment (ROI). Process management is not perceived as a direct saving but more as a factor in long-term productivity gains. The quality of service improvement, where gains are difficult to measure from a financial point of view, is also a factor. This is actually a belief that results from powerful business conditioning that prevails in all aspects of life and is based on ROI and ROCE for everything. This conditioning limits our ability to appreciate certain real benefits of quality. By investing in process, you may not have reduced the quantum of work (you actually shifted the focus from crisis management to planning), but you made the work predictable and reduced the frustration and tension in the work, thereby making a positive impact on the health of employees and improving productivity. People do invest time, money, and effort to maintain good health and still pay a health-insurance premium without worrying about return on capital employed (ROCE) and return on investment (ROI.)

Consider the following facts while setting up a measurement system:

Metrics convert data into knowledge. Process generates operational data, but that data is the raw material for the knowledge—the first step in the data-to-knowledge hierarchy (which is, in ascending order, data, information, knowledge, and wisdom). A well-designed metric will extract knowledge from that data and lead toward the wisdom. You may have collected the data of five thousand tickets and reported SLA achievement on that data, but that is still only information, not knowledge. If you measured repetitive incidents *and* tied those repetitive incidents to a specific problem, then you are talking about knowledge derived from the metric. This knowledge will enable wisdom to eliminate the repetitive incidents.

Metrics dictate people's work. People will do work with the sole consideration of attaining the metrics, because they believe that their performance is measured on achieving the numbers. This is not the right way in a process paradigm, because you should measure process rather than people. However, in the real world, metrics will drive the organization. What gets measured is what gets done; so, metrics should reflect a complete understanding of goals and objectives. So if you are measuring how many incidents a support person resolves, you can expect a sudden increase in the ticket volume—tickets will be created only to get resolved and attain better metrics. For example, I heard about Continental Airlines' measurements to achieve fuel efficiency. They measured pilots for fuel-efficiency targets. Pilots found a variety of ways. One of the easy ways was to compromise the cabin temperature. You make passengers uncomfortable but save fuel!

Align metrics with goals and objectives. Failure to align your metrics with process goals and objectives results in metrics that do not deliver value. One prime example is about the change management operational metrics not being adequately aligned with goal. The most important goal of change-management process is to maintain the integrity of the production environment. That means to ensure that only authorized changes go in production. However, there is absolutely no metric that I have ever seen that will measure how many unauthorized changes were found in a production environment! All change-management process is focused on the RFC life-cycle management that only ensures that submitted RFCs are authorized.

Metrics need maintenance too. Metrics often become obsolete. As the organization achieves higher levels of process and matures, metrics usually require change to keep pace. Good metrics reflect the reality of the current process objectives. When you are releasing some new service or application, you may want to measure some specific parameters till early life cycle or a stability period. But once that period is over, you could retire those measurements, as they are not needed any more.

The metrics should enable better decisions. Metrics are an instrument to gauge the process operation and help make decisions on what can be done to make things better. Do not confine to external metrics only. The real purpose of metrics is to help you make better decisions and to not pin down individuals or punish them. Individual performance metrics tend to cause the measured person to focus on doing what they think management wants, as reflected in the metric. What good is data if I cannot derive knowledge out of it?

Right metrics with accuracy. Metrics should be accurate, timely, and action-able. Data alone does not serve the purpose if it does not tell you what to do. Following are the criteria for good metrics:

1. Align with things that matter to business.

2. Keep it simple.

3. Good enough is perfect.

4. Do less but better—a few good metrics are better than a more exhaustive list of measurements.

5. Use metrics as indicators, not as the conclusion.

6.10 Condition Work-Flow with Policies

When you create a top-level model, you simply define the sub processes. When you drill down the sub process and list the activities in each sub process, you will usually follow the happy path—the straight line from start to finish, with no diversion. However, in many cases there will be diversion, depending upon the conditions and/or policies, and policies may have direct impact on the work-flow. At this stage you will examine those impacts and modify the work-flow. In most cases you will branch out to a different path.

One common example is about the policy about processing a change request during a change-freeze or moratorium. Will you cancel such RFC or delay it or process it through special approval? Depending upon your policy, the work-flow will change.

A similar thing can happen for emergency changes also. In incident-management also, we see lot of work-flow variations based on policies regarding upgrade/downgrade of priority, out-of-scope handling, etc.

6.11 Perform a Process Walk-Through

Now conduct a workshop with process actors and perform a step-by-step demonstration of a process or a step-by-step explanation of it as a novice attempts it. Prompt role players to come out with use cases and map those with your process tasks. This will lead to the discovery of gaps in process and policies or point toward the need for several guidelines.

It is important that you do not drift from the goal. Participants may tend to misdirect you during walk-through: instead of doing the walk-through of your process, they start dictating the process amendments itself to resist the possible change in the process.

6.12 Designing Transaction-Based Processes

When you are designing process for a transaction-based service such as an incident or IMAC, the easiest approach is to think from a transaction-tracking perspective. Each service transaction is short in time scale, and thus status tracking is the core criterion for progress tracking. A process designer can use this criterion to develop the core of the process.

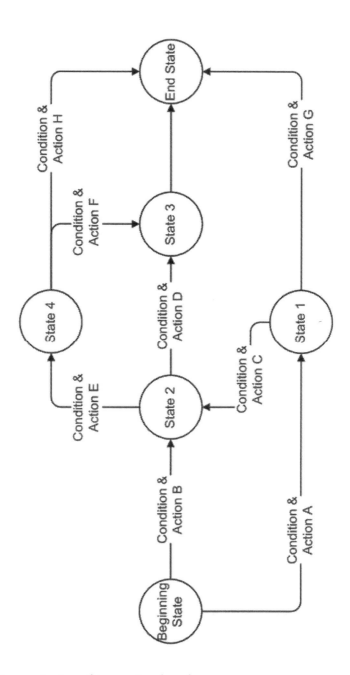

Figure 21: generic view of transaction based process

If a designer just draws a picture of possible states that a transaction will be in, and then connects those states with conditions and actions, then the core part of the process is almost complete. The figure above illustrates the six states of the IMAC process. The arrows indicate the status-transition condition and actions. (That means under what condition and by what action the state will change.) This can be described in a status transition rule table. In the diagram above, conditions and actions contribute to the work-flow and decision-making part of the core process. Depending upon the tracking need, you can create as many states as possible. However, I would like to provide a strong recommendation to limit these states to the optimum value. In my experience, seven states are a universally optimized value. These are the status values in the system where the processes are implemented. I also came across one implementation where a customer had defined twenty-seven states. This allowed tracking precisely where the ticket was at any given point. A closer look revealed that many of these twenty-seven status values were similar. For example, there were seven pending status codes: pending for reasons A, reason B, etc. Similarly there were qualifiers to assigned status, and each qualifier was tagged with an assigned status to create a new status code (assigned for purpose A, assigned for purpose B, etc.). More-logical status design would be to denote the status with a two-tier scheme. It is worthwhile to pay some attention to the implementation consequences when you design such schemes. Most systems would do the measurement based on the time stamp of status value change. With twenty-seven status values, you can collect the twenty-seven time stamps in the life cycle, but, with limited status value, you will not be able collect those many time stamps. For specific measurement, you would be required to create additional time stamps for status reason values as well. Many times a single status value provides the tracking of two states. For example, you do not need three status codes for pending approval, approved, and rejected. You can achieve the same purpose by the consequential status following pending approval. Most probably, approved request will be assigned, and rejected request will be closed. This eliminates the need for approved or rejected status codes.

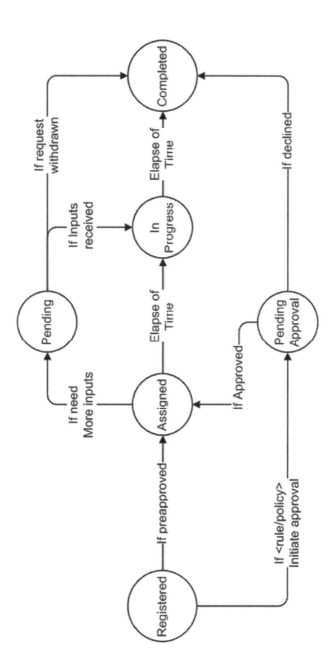

Figure 22: generic view of process illustrated

Service-level-management process is not a transaction-based process but a continuous, open-ended process. SLA tracking for a service transaction is many times referred to as the SLM process but should not be considered as a process by itself. It should be embedded in the process of that transaction-based support itself—for example, incident SLA tracking is primarily a mechanism of monitoring and reporting the response time and resolution time SLA for each incident.

6.13 Design Consideration against Failure

Learning from generic industry experience as well as from one's own past experience brings in good value in design. Generic wisdom is available regarding process failure, and that can be utilized to make appropriate designs and safeguard against failure. The following section talks about such wisdom. Not all the reasons can be addressed in design, and, even if we address some of them, they may not be foolproof; nonetheless, we can still build some protection against failure.

6.13.1 Why Processes Fail

Process are not maintained with business needs.

Our next chapter talks about process maintenance and the needs of process maintenance. Business keeps on changing, and that dictates changes in IT service delivery and support that in turn demands process changes. Regulatory requirements also impact the process. At its face value, process maintenance is not a design issue. But then I can argue that maintainability is one of the design issues. One common example is an approval sub process with a request fulfillment process. It is not unusual that organization policies will amend and demand amendment in approval logic. How was the process designed and implemented? Process amendment on paper does not mean the process has been amended. If the approval process was automated, how easy or difficult would this modification be? These are the design criteria that will make a maintenance job easy or difficult.

Make process structured and modular with an adequate number of sub processes and clear segregation of tasks.

Management is not serious.

Management intent cannot be addressed in design, but management responsibility can be built into the process control. In process management, maturity assessment is one of the benchmarks for improvement. Some maturity tools can "measure" the management intent. There are several symptoms that indicate the management seriousness about the good health of process. Management's value system is one of them. People should be recognized not only for achieving the desired results but also for the method of achieving those results. For example, in a right value system, a service delivery manager will be appreciated for handing a critical incident successfully, but simultaneously he will also be questioned for not preventing the critical incident.

During design, ensure that you have management sponsorship and commitment.

Employees misunderstood or were not aware of the process.

One common theme of misunderstanding is about the guidelines in the process. Most of the time guidelines look good on paper but not meaningful in implementation, because they are very generic. This open to interpretation: guidelines are the source of errors and inconsistencies.

This should be primarily addressed during implementation.

The process is tedious or ineffective.

Tediousness is not only the nature of a particular kind of labor or work but also is associated with boredom. Anything that is not interesting and requires effort will be done with more error and make the process ineffective. In change management, I have to assess the risk, and, in order to perform this task, I need to key in lot of information in RFC that is already available in other systems. If I am not able to import that information, the task will be tedious and automatically become error-prone. Most of the tediousness comes from navigational or performance issues with tools, if the process is implemented in tools. In many cases people adopt paper-based processes or partially paper-based processes that makes tasks tedious: for example, filling in an MS Word form and then attaching it to e-mail.

You must design "implementable" process. For example, in incident management if I am creating a ticket by e-mail, my prescription for data entry will be different based on whether a person is entering data manually or if it is an automatic data transfer.

Participants are not fully and properly trained.

Training is often ignored. In fact, most people treat many process tasks as a matter of common sense. The problem is not the absence of common sense but the variation in the common sense of individuals. For example, interpretation of guidelines under different circumstances requires training to bring in consistent decisions.

This should be primarily addressed during implementation.

There are insufficient tools to follow the processes.

Thomas Carlyle, a famous Scottish satirical writer, once said, "Man is a tool-using animal. Nowhere do you find him without tools; without tools he is nothing, with tools he is all." Yes, he is right, and definitely for IT people. Tools make life easy. If something can be easily done with a tool, then make that tool available.

This also should be primarily addressed during implementation.

There are time constraints.

You must allow the realistic amount of time to do the task in the process. You may anticipate emergencies and provide alternate routes in the process. For example, all IT organizations have emergency change-management processes. You bypass some regular tasks in that. But you do not bypass every task. You still have controls for emergency. It is a most common mistake to believe that emergence implies instant action rather than timely action.

Employees do not understand the importance of the process.

Yet another common problem in IT world: since most of the time people deal with technology and use technology processes, they do not accord due importance to service-management processes. By this ignorance and misunderstanding, they bypass some steps.

This should be primarily addressed during implementation.

Role-mapping is ambiguous.

Every actor in the process must know what task he is expected to perform and in which manner. A person may undertake multiple roles. This usually done during the process implementation—you map the roles to individuals and provide training for that role.

This should be primarily addressed during implementation.

There is a lack of faith in the process.

Faith is about believing in something without asking for the evidence. We demonstrate faith in many aspects of our daily business. When I check in at an airline counter and hand over my baggage, I have full faith that I will receive it on the belt at my destination. I do not challenge airlines systems and processes. We take a step of faith in almost everything in everyday life. Every day when I step out of my home and switch on the ignition of my car, I believe that it will start. I do not plan my day based on what if it did not start. This is a step of faith. We do many things in the way do because we do have faith that by our doing so, it will work. Without faith, life would be miserable. So we do need people to have faith in processes and perform the prescribed tasks faithfully. Another merit of faith is that it helps you to achieve more, simply because we do not waste our energy in inventing solutions to unfound problems! Of course, it is the responsibility of the process manager is to earn that level of faith.

This should be primarily addressed during implementation.

Process itself was inadequately designed for practice.

In past ten years, ITIL phenomenon produced many process consultants who wrote great process, but those processes could not be implemented completely. The main reason was that these consultants were not connected with the gross root of IT operations and ignored the real-life constraints of operations. Such processes became merely the theory to read and not to practice. While it is absolutely necessary to create a theory first, it is also absolutely necessary to bring theory into practice. In fact, *all* technology was first envisioned as theory, and only then could it come to practice. In other words, a validated and relevant theory would make a good foundation of process.

This failure point can be addressed through process stakeholders participating during process design. A workshop is the best instrument to ensure that the process does not remain theory on paper.

There is an inertia of habit and legacy.

Over a period of time, people acquire some behavioral patterns during the regular work with existing processes. These patterns eventually become involuntary and an instinctive way of working. Many processes demand radical change in the way of working. These changes may be necessary for business but become difficult for actors in the processes.

Blindly sticking to the status quo will inhibit your ability to do things better and obtain better results. I am recalling a study that I heard some time back.

Two researchers conducted an experiment with a group of monkeys. Four monkeys were placed in a room that had a tall pole in the center. Suspended from the top of the pole were a bunch of bananas and other exotic fruits. One of the hungry monkeys started to climb the pole to get the bananas. But just as he reached out to grab one, he was blasted with a torrent of cold water from hidden nozzles. He could not withstand the trouble and quickly retreated. He made several attempts, but each time he was tamed by the cold shower. He finally gave up the attempt to get the great food and instead managed with easily available rotten and otherwise compromised food on floor.

Each monkey in turn made a similar attempt, and in turn each was blasted with a torrent of cold water. After making several attempts, all the monkeys concluded that easy but compromised food was the only way to satisfy hunger and survive.

The researchers then removed the shower jets and also removed one of the monkeys from the room and replaced him with a new monkey. As the newcomer began to climb the pole, the other three grabbed him and pulled him down the pole to the ground. After trying to climb the pole several times and being pulled down each time by other "seasoned" or experienced monkeys, the new monkey finally gave up and joined to bandwagon to survive on compromised food.

The researchers replaced the original monkeys one by one, and each time a new monkey was brought in, he would attempt to fetch the banana and would be dragged down by the seasoned monkeys before he could reach the bananas.

Eventually the room was filled with monkeys who had never received the cold shower. Yet none of them would climb the pole. And not one of them knew the reason!

I am afraid that the blind inheritance and adoption of old processes is often the reason of sticking to old ways of working without knowing the reason why: we receive a legacy of habits that we are actively discouraged from questioning.

Organization change-management is one of the key areas during the implementation that can address this issue of habit versus innovation. This is also tied to management's commitment—institutionalization of good process habits is the critical success factor to deal with this potential failure point.

The functional structure of the organization is not adequate.

Since it is the function that executes the process, the adequate functional structure must be in place to run the processes. In fact, the informal functional structure may exist, but if not formalized it will tend to make process itself informal, and that will eventually fail. For example, the service desk as a function is one of the essential requirements for a successful incident-management process. In most organizations it does exist but is not empowered for that function. I invariably come across good service desks, but, without any influence over the support groups, the incident ownership breaks down.

Organization change management is not considered.

Many times a process implementation demands organizational change also. It could be organizational transformation or changes in the ways of working, sometimes radical changes. If those changes are not implemented along with process implementation, then neither change will be successful. So, if I am implementing a new security-management process that imposes some controls on technical-management groups, I must ensure that the technical groups are reconciled to the new working equations.

6.14 *Generally Observed Deficiency*

During my work at various places, I have observed a variety of deficiencies in common processes. One of the biggest issues is the focus on data collection rather than data utilization, and this leads to inefficiencies and deficiency in processes. Some examples of other generic deficiencies follow.

Incident management

There are usually two sources of incidents: those reported by end users and those reported by event-monitoring tools. The first step of incident-management process is entirely different for these originations. When a user reports an incident, the customer, an external person, take the role of "requestor." At the time of closure, explicit consent is obtained from the requestor to close the ticket. By this consent we want to ensure the delivered resolution really did work for the requestor. If the incident is reported by event monitoring, then who will take up the role of requestor? An absolute clarity is required not only to register an incident but also to close the incident.

At the time of registering the incident, a variety of policies have direct influence on the process. One of them is related to the prioritization of the incident. While, in prevailing best practices, prioritization is decided by the combination of impact and urgency, in most organizations prioritization is based on nothing but the severity of an incident. In this scheme, a customer should merely report the symptom, and, based on the guidelines, the help desk should make a judicious decision about the severity of the incident. However, there is often a dispute about the degree of severity. The customer insists a higher value or degree of severity be assigned to obtain the higher level of service. A well-written process will specify a clear guideline to handle disputes between help desks and customers.

Also open to interpretation, vague guidelines are a common deficiency in prioritizing an incident: for example, "Huge business impact: disruption/breakdown of work of multiple people or a business-critical application failure" will not be sufficient unless illustrated by specific examples, such as "Mail/Exchange/Citrix application malfunction at server level," "Catastrophic spread of virus," or "Order booking application <app 1> halted."

Even if the level of clarity is given in the guideline for incident prioritization, the supporting data may not be available; for example, the guideline refers to "Tier 1 business-critical application," but the data or the list of applications may not be available.

There may also be disputes about the scope of the service during the acceptance and registration of the incident. It is important the cover the policy in such cases.

Occasionally, there may be cases where the impact of an incident accessed at the time of registration may not be correct, and after initial diagnosis you may find the impact was different from what it was originally accessed to be. What should be the policy for upgrading or downgrading the impact value during the course of an incident-management life cycle? This is very important, because the measurement and contractual obligations are based on the impact value. Yet another policy is required for keeping the incident status in pending. In most systems the duration of a pending state is not accounted in the SLA measurement. In such systems there is a possibility of abusing the pending status.

In almost all operations, there is something like "critical-incident management," with a variety of processes built around it. Most of the time organizations define the role of critical incident manager but fail to empower him or her. This role demands influence and authority across the technology groups to bring in the resources on demand, but often this is left to a junior person, making process much less effective.

Incident management demands strong policies on some core matters of process, but most often these are ignored.

How will you measure the SLA for variable priority?

How will you handle the dispute on priority?

How do you handle dispute on scope?

How will you prevent the abuse of "pending" status that pauses the SLA?

Problem management

Problem management is the most misunderstood process. Most of the implementations I have seen are actually special-incident management processes. The common mistake that I have seen regards the differentiation between incident and problem. Many times work-around itself is treated as the root cause of an incident. In other words, the problem rarely goes toward the true root cause. The second most-common mistake is about misunderstanding the role of the problem manager and investigator. In almost all implementation that I have seen, the role is never assigned to the right people, and it is reduced to a clerical role. One of the most important obligations that needs to be served by problem-management process is creation and maintenance of a KEDB. However, I rarely found this obligation being served. Technically, for every problem there must be a KEDB record if root cause has been identified. Further, this KEDB record should be active till the time the RFC triggered by the problem management process is closed. In case there is no RFC, the KEDB record will remain active.

In a nutshell, three fundamental concepts of problem management are not adequately understood and implemented:

A problem needs to be qualified before we should invest time and effort in investigation, because not all problems need be investigated.

Even for the problems that have been investigated, we may not have immediate solutions. (RCA identified, but solution not implemented.)

Therefore, we should learn to live with problems; however, there must be an active work-around for every problem we are living with.

All problem-management process implementations talk only about solving the problem. However, a good implementation will also let you learn to live with a problem! This may sound odd, but the truth is that it is not viable to solve every problem, and learning to live with a problem is an important aspect of problem management.

In the application world, we hear the word *defect* very often, and in fact *defect* is another name or terminology for the problem. Ideally all software should be defect-free, but that level of perfection is rarely achieved. This perfection is not merely an IT matter; in many business situations, customers accept deficiencies (and "non-showstopper" defects) and demand an early release. For example the automation of single sign on does not work and user has to provide password each time he accesses a secured content in the across multiple systems.

Besides of this, technology remains the focus of problem management. But in the majority of the cases, the problem is not really with product or technology. It is with the process. If an application failed because data was not available, the root cause will often say "batch job failure." This, in fact, is not the root cause. The root cause is somewhere in the event-management process or in the job configuration itself.

In most organizations, the law of conservation of problems prevails—"problems cannot be eliminated or solved; they can only be transferred from one head to other"—and this law will prevail till you pursue the problem via a well-defined process and methodology under that process to reach the problem's root cause.

Request fulfillment

A successful request-catalog solution will depend on the user profile data. One of the common mistakes people make is that they focus on the service-request (SR) catalog but do not invest in the process of creating and maintaining user profiles. There are compelling reasons to ensure that user profiles are accurately maintained with the tool for effective service management. This is a prerequisite for implementing an SR catalog system. In the SR environment, a good solution should accommodate several types of requests, which will lead to a variety of approval requirements. Some request may require immediate manager's approval only, some requests may require a manager's *and* a manager's manager's approval, and some requests may require a cost-center manager approval.

In order to automate these kinds of approvals, we need strong user-profile management in the process tool to determine the appropriate data source in a particular customer environment and design a solution.

A good solution will also require a strong data strategy. In most organizations, employees have two unique IDs. One is a domain ID only for IT purposes, and the second is an employee/contractor ID for all other purposes. Typically, san ITSM application is designed to use both for different purposes. A good solution would make ITSM system use one unique ID for all purposes and avoid data-management overheads.

The following general points emphasize the need for a strong user-profile management solution:

Dependency of process on user profile: A process may break if a user profile has missing data. For example, a user submits an SR that requires cost-center approval, and the cost-center is not available in the user profile.

Maintaining the integrity of process: A process may deliver a wrong result if executed in a faulty manner. For example, the cost center is available, but it was not correct; therefore, wrong approval was obtained or wrong approval was attempted.

Good service experience to user: User profiles provide personal preferences or attributes that can be used to give a better experience. For example, a VIP flag in a user profile enables the service provider to accord higher importance to that customer.

Smooth operation of process: for example, a user's building and cubicle location will enable onsite service to be provided more effectively.

Quality of customer service: for example, communication throughout the service transaction will use the contact data from the user profile.

Help in workload management: for example, based on the physical location information derived from the profile, you can optimize multiple customer visits and improve logistics of service delivery.

Compliance help: you can track the privileges assigned to a user and support Sarbanes Oxley (SOX) compliance.

A second but no less important aspect is to implement the process for managing the service catalog itself. No catalog will be static, and it will change with business need. Some organizations understand catalog maintenance: they do it like content management. Catalog management is quite different than content management.

Change management

What is considered as "change" is not often very well defined. In many organizations the a change-management process controls the rebooting of a server, although a reboot is not a change that accords with the recognized definition of a change. It is OK to use the process as an easy instrument to control the reboot, but those kinds of items should be listed as exceptions. I would normally recommend very clearly defining what is considered as a change and also what is not considered as change. A policy statement such as "Routine housekeeping activities that do not alter operating systems, utilities, or applications, but are designed to maintain the overall health and performance of the computing environment" would be sufficient in the process document but must be clearly illustrated in implementation with an environment-specific example. You should give more-specific examples, such as defragmentation of disk drives, purging log files, or rebuilding database indexes.

Just what triggers change management is one of the questions that is inadequately answered in most implementations. Many organizations treat change controls only to maintain the integrity of the production environment. That means whatever happens before that change is not monitored. While this may work for the infrastructure layer, it is definitely not suitable for application changes. This leads to implementation of two change-management processes—one for infrastructure and one for application. Application changes traverse through multiple environments and are tracked throughout their life cycle. Infrastructure changes do not have "development" work, but they still need to be tested. I prefer to have one single process with different points of entry in the process cycle.

Yet other inconsistencies in change management are in the treatment of emergency changes. A common practice is to trigger an emergency change that is required to resolve a critical incident, but there is no enforcement. Also, unqualified and untested changes make their way through this weakness. The policy itself is not weak, but implementation is often weak.

Risk assessment of changes is very often inadequate. Most of the time "technical" people perform the risk assessment: that itself is a risk. Besides this, the risks are often noted without supporting document and methodology. The risks are based on what a person thinks rather than what he knows—the data is usually not available or analyzed sufficiently when available. I usually address this by incorporating risks criteria and guidelines to bring in consistency of assessment across groups and individuals.

Despite all the precautions and measures, changes may still fail in production. While the process needs to be designed to eliminate the chance of failed changes, it also needs to provision for the policies about failed changes. The criteria of success or partial success (and thus partial failure) are not adequately established in many change-management processes. Also, the policies around failed changes (partially failed and completely failed) are often not clear and crisp.

Change management is also mixed up with release management. The fundamental concept that every release is a change, but every change is not a release, is not understood very well.

Configuration management and CMDB

One of very common scenarios that I have come across is the proud statement of several IT organizations about "CMDB implementation" that they have done. First of all, CMDB is a database and does not have value without a configuration-management process. In almost all cases, I noted that they implemented a tool but not a process. CMDB and configuration management are not same. CMDB is a database, and configuration management is the control process built around CMDB to maintain the accuracy, currency, and integrity of the data in the CMDB.

Similarly, discovery and data-filling are not a CMDB creation. A discovery tool does not discover all the data that may be required to create a CMDB, and lot of "data preparation" is required before you can actually use discovered data. Discovery is a very small part of a real CMDB project.

Also, integration of a discovery tool and CMDB is not configuration management; a lot of control processes must have built-in tools before you do this, and you also need to take care of other data that is not discovered. A meaningful CMDB proposition should have at least three elements:

1. Design—the design of a data model and CMDB architecture will be driven by the purpose of the CMDB.

2. CMDB baseline creation—identifies multiple data sources, discovery, data preparation, and data loading.

3. Control of process design and implementation.

In any CMDB implementation, the consulting and implementation cost will be many times the cost of tools.

Mixing asset management and configuration management

Similarly, I also come across lot of misconception around asset management and its getting mixed up with configuration management, primarily because of tools mixing them up. The irony is that ITIL V3 even contributed this misconception with its "Service Asset and Configuration Management" process in ITIL v3. I take this opportunity to make the concept clear that an asset DB and a CMDB are not the same.

Asset is a hardware product or software license that needs to be managed, because it has some *economic value,* and asset DB is the database that provides information about IT assets. An asset DB will have information about *economic attributes* such as cost, depreciation, contract, and purchase date but *no* information about relationships with other assets.

Configuration item is a component of IT infrastructure that need to be managed because it has impact on IT service. CMDB will have information about technical attributes/configurations such as host name, IP address, and relationship with other CI but *no* information about economic value.

An asset may or may not be a CI; conversely, a CI may or may not be an asset. Asset DBs and CMDBs may share some common items—for example, data center devices—but different attributes. Some items may be included only in an asset DB but not in a CMDB: for example, end-user devices, and software licenses.

Some items may be included only in a CMDB but not in an asset DB: for example, a logical system (cluster and virtual machine but note—in cloud computing, a virtual machine is a candidate for asset item as well).

Asset life cycle is significantly longer. (A server can exist in asset DB in status "in stock," but will not exist in a CMDB, till the asset status transits to "deployed"; similarly, a decommissioned asset will not exist in a CMDB but exists in an asset DB).

Asset-management processes and configuration-management processes are not the same. Asset-management process is the **control process** build around an *asset DB* and deals with accounting, purchase, depreciation, and disposal processes. Configuration management process is the control process around *CMDB* and deals with technical configuration changes, such as port change or route change and relationship changes.

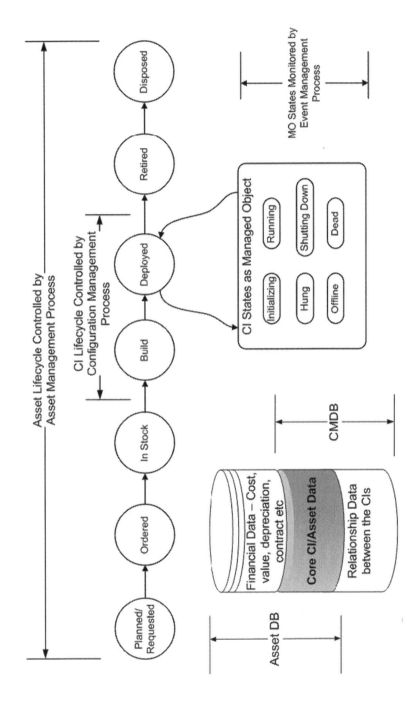

Asset discovery is *not* an asset-management process. Typical asset-management proposals (excluding software) will have two basic elements:

1. Asset DB creation

2. Development and implementation of asset-management process

While the first part is much simpler, the second part is much more complex than configuration-management process. The cost of implementing asset-Management process is significantly higher than tool cost. The typical asset life cycle includes the following:

1. Procuring IT assets

    a. Identifying requirements

    b. Requesting IT asset-procurement service

    c. Processing procurement information requests

    d. Processing IT asset requests

    e. Tracking purchase orders

2. Receiving IT assets

    a. Asset tag generation

    b. Managing IT asset inventory

    c. Updating IT asset inventory

    d. Performing / auditing inventory

    e. Resolving inventory exceptions

3. Managing IT asset operations

    a. Monitoring IT asset operations (e.g., install, maintain, support)

    b. Handling IT asset hardware life-cycle events (changes, upgrades, etc.)

    c. Warranties and maintenance contracts

    d. Asset refresh planning

4. Managing IT asset accounting

   a. Depreciation and value tracking

   b. Charge back

   c. Managing accounts payable

5. Returning / Disposing IT assets

   a. Decommissioning assets

   b. Preparing IT assets for return or disposal

   c. Returning IT assets

   d. Disposing IT assets

A comprehensive asset-management process will serve a variety of goals, and you need to focus on your goals. If your goal is CAPEX control, focus on the first sub process; if your goal is good service delivery, focus on the third and fourth sub processes. If your goal is OPEX control, focus on the fifth sub process; and if you want compliance, then focus on the sixth sub process.

If the scope includes software, consider that asset-management software is comprehensive and very complex and typically includes the following:

1. Selection, standardization, and approval for software products (especially architectural and compatibility consideration of the environment)

2. Purchasing or otherwise obtaining software, such as downloading it for use

3. Managing software installations, licenses, and contracts, including proof of ownership (very complex because of variety of licensing schemes, such as pay-by-use or other kinds of end user license agreement (ELA))

4. Reclaiming licensed software for reuse (harvesting process)

5. Creating and maintaining a definitive software library (DSL)

6. Legal compliance and preventing unauthorized use

7. Most asset-management software addresses only a part of above processes.

Availability management process

Many IT organizations do not have a specific process for availability management and hope that higher levels of availability will occur with the introduction of new and improved hardware. While fault-resistant hardware and data sharing can help availability, the root of poor availability can typically be found primarily in two areas: IT processes and application design.

Application design is one aspect of availability management that is often forgotten. If the application is not written and designed for a high-availability environment, obtaining availability goals would be much more complicated in today's dynamic business environment. This is often missed in process.

A strong focus on a few supporting processes that are thoroughly defined and implemented can significantly improve availability. Availability management is a specific set of interrelated IT processes and tools that need to be viewed and managed from a single vantage point in order to maintain the highest service delivery possible. IT processes such as change management and backup-and-recovery management have a direct impact on availability, while other processes, such as managing configuration changes, may have only an indirect impact. Following are the specific supporting processes and their role to support availability:

Establish availability requirements and availability SLA—this is in the scope of service-level management process.

Establish availability monitoring and take corrective actions for events of unavailability—this is in the scope of event management, incident management, and problem management.

Measure and report availability against availability SLA—this is in the scope of the SLM process.

Initiate improvement for availability—this is in scope of the CSIP process.

The following key activities are most often ignored in the availability-management process:

1. Availability risk assessment and management

2. Implementing cost-justifiable countermeasures

3. Event-management process

Event management as a formal process is rarely recognized and implemented in most IT organizations. What exists in the name of event management is the monitoring tool implementation. Even if I consider this as their event management process, I still find several deficiencies.

Most of the implementations are based on the standard threshold parameters—tool people will produce some template that will record some parameter to configure the monitoring threshold. The correct threshold value should be derived from the health model of the object. For example, if a server is being used as file server, then 25 percent CPU utilization could be an alarm; however, if the server is being used for transaction processing, then 75 percent CPU utilization could be normal. If you are monitoring both against the same parameter, you will be either producing false alerts or missing genuine alerts.

Another common issue is the inability to differentiate among events, alarms, and incidents. For example, that a file system is 95 percent full is not an incident, because the application is still running. (Discard the logic that it has the potential to create service disruption, because you would then be treating huge numbers of events as incidents.) To open an "automatic ticket" in a help-desk tool is a very common mistake for unqualified events. People do so because it can be done and because vendors say so.

Service-level management (SLM) process

Most of the SLM processes' implementations are limited to measurement and reporting of SLA. Where is the benchmarking of service-level requirements against SLAs? Where is benchmarking of delivery capabilities against SLR?

In ITIL V2 even the development and maintenance of a service catalog was in an SLM process, and that has been excluded in V3—maybe people are not doing it anyway, so ITIL removed it to make it easy!

While SLAs are defined, the measurement logic is left wide open for interpretation. OLA is frequently ignored; that leaves a big crack in SLA. I have seen some SLAs during my assessment work that demand application availability more than system availability on which the application is running!

Knowledge management (KM)

One of the biggest failures of IT organizations is about differentiating between knowledge and data. Most of the time, data is treated as knowledge, and that directly impacts the usability and the purpose of knowledge management.

Invariably, knowledge management is deemed to be the deployment of collaborative applications. Deployment of technology such as groupware application, collaborative applications, data mining, and data warehousing applications is *not* knowledge management. Technology does not create knowledge. It only helps and facilitates managing the knowledge. In fact, the concept of KM was born because the technology to manage it has become affordable. KM is the process of managing the entire life cycle of the knowledge: from developing/discovering the knowledge from raw data, storing it, and distributing it to the people in the organization for business goals.

Customer satisfaction (CSAT)

This one of the most misunderstood areas and lacks the service focus in most IT operations. While customer-satisfaction measurement is one of the best tools available for real service improvement, it is also the most underutilized tool.

We all know customer satisfaction is one of the key metrics in all IT service outsourcing contracts, and we must have some mechanism to find out whether our customers are satisfied. Varieties of measurements are established, but they lack the fundamentals.

Most measurements are based on the responses to a few questions on the survey that is embedded into the incident-management process. In fact, it is a very good idea to do so, but that is where the goodness or value of this idea ends. The closure moments of a service-support transaction offer an opportunity to solicit the feedback, but use this opportunity in such a way that it goes beyond the narrow purpose of measuring the service desk or the success of that transaction alone. What happens most often is that the performance of the service desk is judged based on the customer-satisfaction (CSAT) measurements. Customer response on surveys should be deemed to be the response to *all* service delivery and service support rather than viewing it just as the feedback for the service desk. In fact, the customer may be dissatisfied because of multiple reasons. Here are a few scenarios:

A customer reported an incident that was resolved in time, and the solution did work as expected. In the entire process, his call was answered promptly; the incident was promptly diagnosed as a virus attack on his laptop. The technician took prompt action and cleaned the virus; resolution was delivered in a timely manner, and the solution worked perfectly. Yet the customer responded in the survey response that he was dissatisfied. The reason for his dissatisfaction was that the virus entered the system at all when there were all kind of protections that were installed and maintained by corporate IT! This is a clear failure of the security-management process.

In another situation several users were dissatisfied when an e-mail server was down. All these customers made desperate calls to the service desk, which promptly responded and assigned the ticket to the mail server team and regularly updated the user community about the progress. Finally, when the e-mail was restored within the SLA time, a satisfaction survey response was sent to each user who had created the ticket via phone or web. While some of them appreciated that they were kept informed about the progress, several were dissatisfied and commented that e-mail was not reliable. A failure of availability-management process caused the customer dissatisfaction.

Many times the help desk comes across customer calls and web tickets reporting a slow performance of a system, network, or application. Quite possibly the slowdown is because of a seasonal effect on the usage, and the issue disappears on its own. However, before it gets automatically resolved, it leaves behind the traces of customer dissatisfaction on the closure of incident tickets. This, in fact, is the failure of a capacity-management process that failed to account for the seasonal demand in application sizing or network bandwidth sizing.

Many times customers expect response time or resolution time better than what SLA has contracted for. In such cases, even if you resolve an incident within your SLA time limit, the customer will still not be happy. Since it is the responsibility of the service-level management process to communicate the SLA to all service users, we can say that this process needs to be improved if users are dissatisfied with the SLA. Similarly, a bad incident-management process will delay resolution, thereby producing customer dissatisfaction.

Customer satisfaction is more a matter of meeting or exceeding customer expectations rather than the actual, contracted service levels. It is possible that we exceed the SLA but still fail on customer satisfaction because the customer's expectation was higher than the SLA; conversely, we could receive customer appreciation for the service that has breached the SLA just by managing the expectation appropriately. If we do not do anything to set the expectation, then it will be set by default, and that may impact customer satisfaction. Expectations should be managed by an SLA process and dynamically supported by an incident-management process.

In order to avoid customer dissatisfaction due to wrong expectation, it is important to proactively set up the right expectation. One of the easy methods to do so is to communicate the expected resolution time on the basis of contracted service levels at the time of communicating the ticket number. This can be automated in the system.

Response should be analyzed in the context of the entire set of data—the transaction data that invoked the survey as well as the indirectly related data.

Is anything more important than customer satisfaction?

Every organization claims that customer satisfaction is their most important motto. (The trueness of this claim can be judged from the real practice—how far you are willing to go to satisfy customers, especially if there are financial consequences. In practice you will see that financials are even more important than customer satisfaction.)

In the service industry, the customer loyalty is far more important than customer satisfaction. If you have a loyal customer, you have everything. The repeat and continued business is assured from loyalty. Of course, one can argue that loyalty is the result of continued and sustained customer satisfaction, but that satisfaction is not necessary. Learn from the airlines' business model in which millions of dollars are spent to run a loyalty program and "buy" loyal customers. You will realize that not all loyal customers are satisfied, but still they give repeat business to the airline. Surely, if I win customer loyalty, I do not need customer satisfaction; loyalty is always more important than satisfaction—at least for business purposes. Customer satisfaction may lead to customer loyalty, but not necessarily. A dissatisfied customer can stay loyal and continue to do business with you. (That relationship may be fragile, though.) However, there are methods and techniques in the market economy that create incentives for dissatisfied customers to stay loyal. Airlines mileage programs are one such example.

So I would focus more on the loyalty and sideline customer satisfaction. However, in the IT service-management business, this rule cannot be applied, because we do have captive customers, so their "loyalty" is enforced. Therefore, customer satisfaction automatically becomes the next most-important thing.

Furthermore, for an IT service-improvement agenda, customer satisfaction does not deliver much feedback or action items for the improvement. The real improvement agenda and feedback and action items come from the customer *dis*satisfaction. Therefore, the measurement of customer dissatisfaction becomes more important than customer satisfaction itself.

The best time to conduct a customer satisfaction survey is when the experience is fresh in their minds. If we wait to conduct a survey, the customer's response may be less accurate. He or she may have forgotten some of the details. So, the approach should be to collect the response within a week of completing the service transaction, as we want to do the survey before the memory of the experience fades away. The two most common mistakes or deficiency in this area are as follows:

The kind of questions people ask. "Was the technician knowledgeable?" is, though, the most common question that I have seen in these implementations, but it is an insane question to ask. Are you measuring the knowledge of technician, or you are measuring customer satisfaction? How you can rely on the judgment of an end user on the technical skill of the technician? How do you know that he or she is qualified to measure the knowledge of the technician? What is the purpose of asking such a question? Is the customer interested in the knowledge of technician—or good service? A highly knowledgeable person does not guarantee the production of good service. Even if we believe it does, the total contribution of knowledge toward customer satisfaction is such a small part that to assess that would waste an opportunity to obtain feedback.

The interpretation that is derived from the response. The conclusion you draw from the response is an even larger problem. So if an end user stated that the technician was not knowledgeable, then you would conclude that the person requires training. Why would you not conclude that the right person is in the wrong job? Or why would you not conclude that the manager who hired him did the mistake, and that the manager was less qualified than the user to assess the knowledge of the technician? Even if the conclusion on training is correct, and you train the person, you still cannot guarantee that it will produce customer satisfaction.

The problem with some common methods of surveying customer satisfaction, then, is that we collect unreliable data and then make incorrect conclusions.

So what is the right thing to do?

Satisfaction is highly subjective and personal. Therefore, do not attempt to measure individual factors (such as a technician's skill) externally, through the customer. Instead, measure the satisfaction level as determined by the customer himself—the end result. Therefore only one question will suffice—how much you were satisfied with service?

Further, collect the data on dissatisfaction reasons, and then analyze it correctly. I have seen service desks being judged by customer-satisfaction measurements. The fact is that the customer experience is the interpretation of service as a whole and must be interpreted in that context:

If CSAT is bad because of repeat failures, then it is failure of problem management, not the service desk.

If CSAT is bad because of performance/response time (application or network), then it is failure of capacity-management process, not the service desk.

If CSAT is bad because the customer was expecting faster-than-SLA service, then it is failure of SLM process, not the service desk.

If CSAT is bad because the quality of the solution is bad, then it is failure of problem-management process, not the service desk.

If CSAT is bad because of a timeliness issue, then it is failure of incident-management process, not the service desk.

If CSAT is bad because service was not reliable, then it is the failure of availability-management process, not the service desk.

Service desk

A service desk is the prime customer-facing function in an IT organization. The need for a "strategic" service desk has been promoted in several forums and well recognized by all across the industry at all levels. However, when it comes to practice, this is rarely adopted. This is less a deficiency and more a hypocrisy. I invariably see all service desks at operational level, not even at tactical level. In various discussions, though, all IT management want to claim that they have a "service desk."

During my maturity-assessment exercise, I seek evidences that will support the claim of strategic service desk, but I rarely find. The service desk is entrusted with the responsibilities of managing the incident life cycle and critical incident life cycle, but they do not have influence over resolution groups. How you can bring in the rule of law and order without teeth?

For real users, the service desk has the functions that can help to obtain the full value of technology for end customers. But unfortunately that is the place where there is maximum cost-cutting, and it is deemed to be the lowest rank in the IT organization. Almost everywhere the story is the same but not always. One of the most astonishing examples I came across of an empowered service desk is worth mentioning. In this organization, every month, the CIO came to the service desk and spent one hour in the role of a service desk agent. He actually takes the call and creates the ticket. This gives him the opportunity to understand what exactly is reaching to the end customers, and whether all the services produced and delivered by application and infrastructure are usable or not, and to what extent they are usable. The service desk is the stage that provides an opportunity to listen to the customer.

I am sure this CIO would be taking lot of input to develop the IT strategy to serve the purpose of end customers.

7 QUICK ILLUSTRATION OF DESIGN APPROACH

Now let me apply these principles and design a process. I am choosing "patch-management process" to illustrate this approach. There are three reasons to select this process:

It is among the most critical processes in the IT world, so some guidance on this will be useful for readers of this book.

This is not stated as a separate process in ITIL, but in most organizations it is recognized as a separate and prime process and is not conditioned by ITIL, although the principles of release management do apply.

The characteristic of patch-management process is transactional as well as cyclic, and this will provide additional insight to a design approach.

This section is not about the development of patch-management process but an illustration of a method to develop a patch-management process. So you will see the direction with some basic process information. The complete process as an outcome of this illustration is included in the annexure of this book.

7.1 Define the Process Environment

Let me create a hypothetical environment: A company has its primary data center in location A and a secondary data center in location B. The primary data center has about fifteen hundred servers, and the secondary data center has about five hundred servers. There is a server-management group who is adequately staffed to maintain these servers. The IT organization has the required functional groups, such as security and audit. The organization also has an adequate level of supporting processes, such as change management and configuration management. There are adequate tools available for patch deployment, and tools are maintained as well.

7.1.1 Scope Clarity

Hypothetically, after a few discussions and debates, we concluded that the scope is limited to a Windows environment only.

7.2 Define the Approach

The next question is about whether to establish a new patch management or reengineer the existing process, I am taking a greenfield approach based on the following input provided by the sponsor:

There are several silos, each pursuing its own process, and therefore there is not a single official process to reengineer.

The organization is looking for a future option of outsourcing "patch management" as a service. So the organization will own this process, and a third party will operate.

The new process will be deployed in phases, piloting with one group and then adopted corporation-wide.

7.3   Establish a Foundation

We established the foundation during a series of meetings and workshop and documented the following:

The executive sponsor is the chief information security officer, a fairly influential person, to make the project successful.

The named process owner was identified as the security manager—another advantage, as we shall see that the process owner has stakes in the process.

Goal and scope has been identified and agreed upon that appears in the documents.

Customers who this process will serve—the server owner's application owners have been involved and identified.

7.4   Process Template

I will use the template as described in an earlier section 5.5.

7.5   Create a Top-Level Model

When I think of a top-level model for patch management process, I come out with four major sub processes:

- Patch identification and qualification
- Patch testing
- Approval and deployment
- Audit and assessment

We also know this organization has a change-management process, and every patch-application deployment has to go through change control; and, in fact, patch management is a form of release management and deployment. Patch-management is not a one-time activity; it is cyclic in nature and the same transactional process needs to be repeated at regular intervals. The top-level model is designed to address what is required from the process. As you can see, in addition to deploying the patch, we also need to ensure that the environment is current; hence, audit and assessment is added as one of the sub process. With this consideration my top-level model will look like the diagram below:

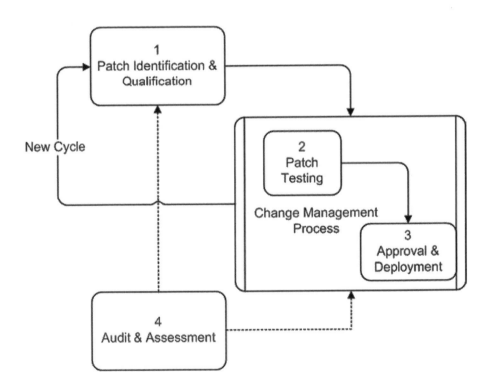

Figure 23: Top level process for patch management

Having established this model, I would give a form of process to this model by adding the roles. A model by which to process overview is arrived at by answering one question: "Who will do what?" When I add roles, I will represent them in swim lanes to give a formal process structure, and this will become my process overview, as below:

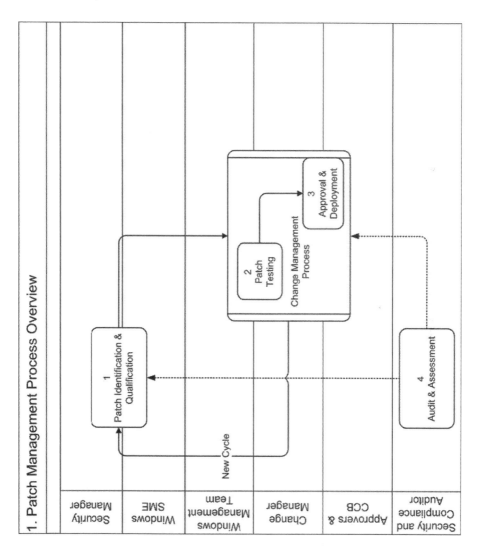

Figure 24: Patch management overview

At this time I do not need to worry about whether people are there or not; the role can be assigned during implementation. In fact, role assignment is a major part of implementation. As you see here, I have come up with six major roles:

1. Security manager

2. Window SME

3. Window management team

4. Change manager

5. Approvers and change Control Board/Change Advisory board (CCB/ CAB)

6. Security and compliance auditor

This automatically leads to the conclusion that the existence of a sound change-management process is a prerequisite for a sound patch-management process. Now I am ready to expand the process overview.

7.6 Drill in the Blocks and Expand

7.6.1 Document the Background

Microsoft releases security patches on the second Tuesday of the month, and this is usually called Patch Tuesday and is deemed to be the start of patch-management process in most organizations. (There is also "Exploit Wednesday" or "Day Zero," when attacks may be launched against the newly announced vulnerabilities.) Starting with Windows 98, Microsoft included a "Windows Update" system that would check for patches to Windows and its components, which Microsoft would release intermittently. With the release of Microsoft Update, this system also checks for updates to other Microsoft products, such as Office, Visual Studio, and SQL Server.

The regular Patch Tuesday begins at 17:00 UTC (Coordinated Universal Time). Sometimes there is an emergency Patch Tuesday, fourteen days after the regular Patch Tuesday. There are also updates that are published daily (e.g., definitions for Windows Defender and Microsoft Security Essentials) or irregularly. Although not a declared trend, according to historical observations, Microsoft has a pattern of releasing a larger number of updates in even-numbered months and fewer in odd-numbered months.

7.6.2   Patch Identification and Qualification

We are at the beginning of the process now. How do we start? The answer will also deliver the information about the process components, trigger, and input. I may ask the questions to the role-players at this point and gather the answer, or I may use my knowledge to answer. In the latter case, it will still be verified during the process walk-through, whether I assumed correct inputs or not. At this time, I have the following answers:

Microsoft releases the patch on every second Tuesday of the month, so an e-mail notification from Microsoft on each second Tuesday will be my trigger and input.

Proactively, the security manager and Windows SME may subscribe to free services of patch alerts, such as patchmanagement.org, or they may research and initiate their own action.

The notification and proactive research will tell you the patch level and its description, but you also need to compare it with your current patch level. This information must be maintained somewhere, and this would be a prerequisite of patch-management process.

Configuration details of each server ought to be maintained in CMDB, so this data input will come from CMDB. This makes my inputs complete for sub process 1, activity 1.

Now think of what you will do after receiving the patch notification and comparing it to your current patch level. This automatically leads to several tasks that I have listed in the following diagram.

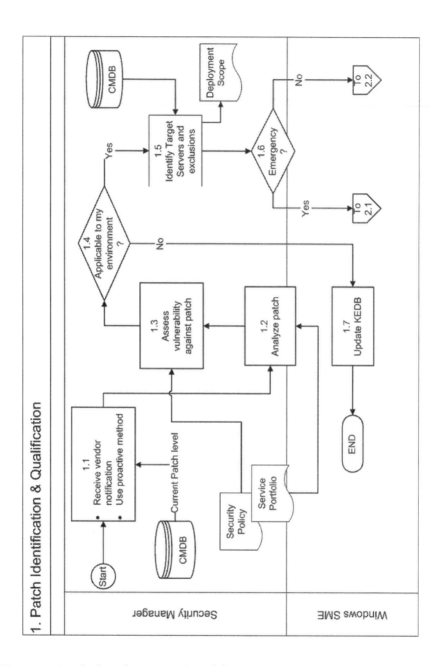

Figure 25: Patch identification and qualification

So my sub process is broken down into five activities, two decision points, and three inputs. There will be some output also at the end of each of the activities.

The next concern about policy and guidelines at this stage is that, as a general rule, you will need policies and guidelines for all decision-making points. In this process the first decision-making point is about the applicability of the patch, so I will need some policies and guidelines that will enable me to take the right decision of yes or no. A typical policy statement follows: "Applicability of patch will be decided based on the current configuration as well as future configurations that are envisaged in the portfolio pipeline in under development state." As soon as I make this policy statement, I would be required to add "service portfolio" along with CMDB as the input requirements.

The second decision point is about whether the patch is considered emergency or non-emergency, so you shall need a clear policy statement behind it. My typical suggested policy statement would be, if it is a critical security threat, then it should be taken as an emergency.

In addition to policies and guidelines for decision points in the sub process, you may require additional policies and guidelines for certain tasks. For example, in this sub process, activity 1.5 will require some guidelines. You can also argue that every activity will require some or other kind of guidelines, but I will leave it to the discretion of the process designer as to what should be considered commonsense and does not require policy or guideline. In any case, the process also assumes that the role-player has an adequate level of skill and knowledge to perform that activity.

Following the above direction, you will be able to establish the policies, guidelines, outputs, and even procedures for this sub process. One important thing to remember: unless you have not established the output of this sub process, you will not be able to start the next sub process. In this case we do have the following outputs:

The information about the patch in KEDB, which tells us that we are living without this patch. Technically it may not be an error, but I recommend retaining it in KEDB to serve a future purpose. Should the criteria for the patch change, we will have this ready information about what patches to consider.

Data to plan patch testing—what patch, which servers to include, and which servers to exclude

Clear flag of timing of next actions

7.7   Develop Policies and Guidelines

During the drilling down of a sub process, we shall be able to derive the policies and guidelines and include them in the process document. However, there will be some process-level policies and guidelines that will not come from pondering on the sub-process activities. For example, in this case the cycle-time policies. Do you align your cycle time with some other factors within the organization or dictate them from this process?

Also, some of the policies will be inherited from the change-management process:

Moratorium policy in change management—whether to apply for patch or not

Emergency and non-emergency change

It is mandatory to test and produce evidence before deployment in production.

As to what extent you should detail these policies, there is absolutely no rule. As I said earlier, many policies and guidelines may be a matter of common sense.

7.8 Condition Work-Flow with Policies

Conditioning work-flow with policies is also done during walk-through. This is preliminary conditioning during development itself to determine if work-flow alters based on policy. One example is that a policy on testing could demand identical test environments, but that may not be available. In that case the work-flow will branch out to different paths that may not have been originally included in the activity list.

7.9 Develop Other Process Components

Guided by the above cycle and with a well-structured template, I am now able to add the other components, which include roles and responsibilities, measurement and reporting, relationship with other processes, and so on.

7.10 Perform a Process Walk-Through and Update

I would organize a workshop with all the role-players, perform the walk-through with the use cases provided by participants, and relate it to their day-to-day operations.

7.11 Design Consideration against Failure

Patch management should be designed in such a manner that the process is maintainable. By making it modular and outsourcing the test and deployment completely to change-management process, it will remain current.

Because of sponsorship from chief information security officer (CISO), the seriousness of management is evident, and it will keep the process focused.

By defining the cycle time that is based on the industry practices, we are eliminating time-constraint miscalculations.

7.12 Participation from Customers

The customers are the internal IT people who use this process to produce their services (availability, security, etc.); hence, they must be involved in the process-design workshops, discussions, and walk-throughs.

8 ILLUSTRATION OF PROCESS OVERHAULING

In many organizations, some processes have grown beyond the IT organization's ability to effectively manage them. Aggressively rationalizing process strategies and overhauling process can help create solutions that will meet changing business requirements as well as the constraints of the IT budget. Process overhauling is a thorough renewal of processes—a kind of remake—that will result in processes significantly different than the original. Overhauling is very high degree of process reengineering. One of the common examples I will offer is about a service-requests process that needs overhauling, and this section provides an approach.

8.1 Business Scenario

There are several hundred service requests existing in an IT service catalog in different forms. Each service request has its own formal or informal process behind it. These processes are handled with different tools, partially or completely. The goal of the service-request process overhauling is to

1. consolidate the discrete and isolated processes and bring them under a common global process,

2. identify duplicate/redundant processes and unify/merge them,

3. optimize the number of processes without impact on request fulfillment, and

4. improve the processes for efficiency and effectiveness.

This overhauling approach is comprised of three sequential stages:

Preparation Stage: During this stage, collect the information about the existing service requests and the processes behind them. There will be some preparation work before we can proceed to the next stage.

Process Analysis Stage: During this stage, processes will be analyzed at a macro level to build the foundation for process-engineering work at the next stage. Identification of duplicity and redundancy at the process level will happen at this stage, and a consolidated, new SR list will be developed.

Process Synthesis Stage: During this stage, some analysis is still done at the micro level, but mainly the stage focuses on constructing and reengineering the process with the existing policy. New requirements could be included at this stage, but the prime inputs will be the components of existing processes.

These stages are explained in details in subsequent sections.

8.2 Preparation

This requires continuous participation from process owners/stakeholders.

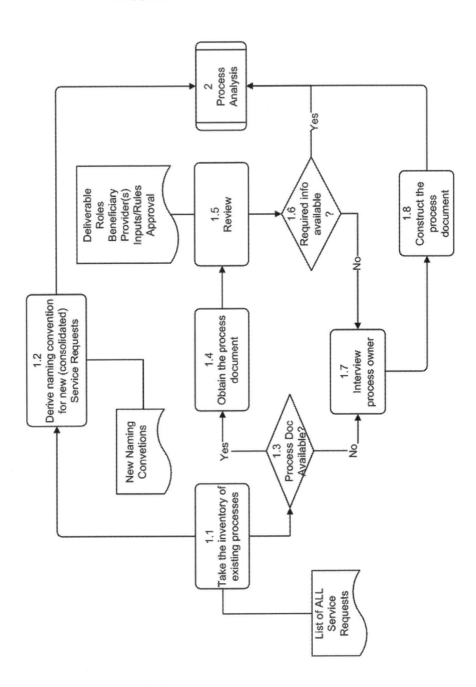

Figure 26: process overhauling preparation

Preparation starts with taking inventory of existing service-request processes. The number of SR processes in any organization will vary depending upon the size of the organization, but in most the organizations there are around fifty common processes that normally service desk and data center people use. In savvy IT organizations, it could be one hundred. After you take up the inventory, you will know the exact number you are dealing with. You should collect the process-specific document for each of these listed processes. It will not be unusual if that document is nonexistent. In other words, the process must be running in some tool, but there was no document created. You may also come across the situation that each of the documents is in a different form and has different details.

If the document does not exist, you will interview the process owner and construct the process from the verbal description of the process owner. Even if the process document exists, it may not have adequate information to analyze, and you may still complete the process.

The inventory list will give you the opportunity to examine the existing service names. You should expect lot of inconsistency in naming conventions. But you should treat all these names as raw materials to build logical and consistent naming conventions for the consolidated service-request catalog.

8.3 Process Analysis

Many service requests will be a duplicate or variant of a single service request or process. The variations can be based on geography or towers. For example, "privileged access for Unix server" and "administrative access for Windows server" are the same kind of service request but can be listed as two different requests. We shall review the process by considering the following questions:

What are the deliverables?

Who is the beneficiary?

Who is the provider of that service?

Most of the processes can be grouped into a single set based on the above aspect. You may also consider "internal" service requests, which are internal to IT (for example, privileged access to servers, data center card key, etc.) or "external" service request, which are end-user-facing (for example, install new software on desktop/laptop, or provide a new desktop/laptop).

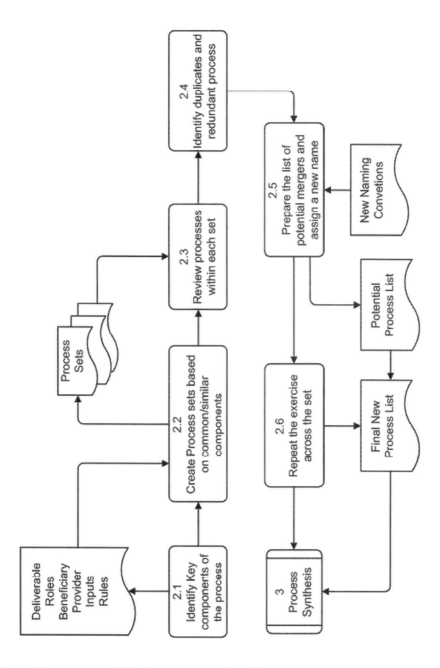

Figure 27: process analysis for process overhauling

You will prepare the process sets based on these attributes and identify the duplicate/redundant process within each set. We shall also do the same identification across the set. For example, user account requests and privileged account requests may be considered similar, even though they may fall in different sets of "internal" and "external."

8.4 Process Synthesis

Process synthesis is a process design and engineering work and task are explained in the diagram below:

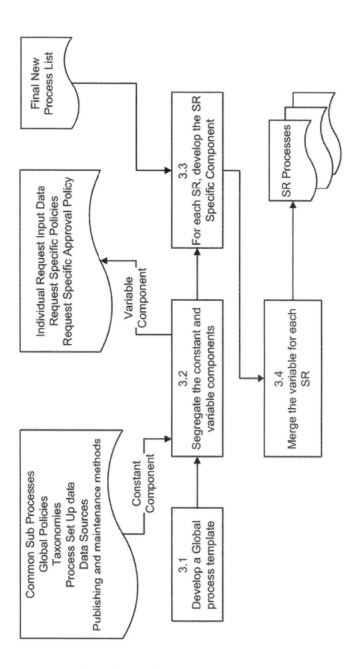

Figure 28: process synthesis for overhauling

When you start the process synthesis, you already have the naming conventions and the final service-request list. At this time you will develop a global process template. This template will depict a common umbrella process for all service requests and will include five sub processes:

1. Request submission

2. Request verification and approval, if required

3. Request assignment and multiple task assignment, if required

4. Work performance

5. Delivery, acceptance, and closure

Now when you drill down the global sub process, you will be able to identify the constant component and variable component. There will be global policies; for example, you may state that a request will be accepted only from the web portal, and no telephonic request will be accepted. This policy applies to all service requests. Similarly, taxonomy, process set of data, and a global work-flow as defined by the sub processes earlier will be the common components. Variable components will include individual request input data—for example, in the first sub process of a request submission, the request data for a new laptop would be the laptop model, add-on options, and shipping address. However, if the request is for privileged access on a server, then probably the input data will demand the server name. Similarly, another variable component is policies. The policy for accepting the privileged access request will be very specific to that process only and will not be applicable to any other service-request process. Approval policy is yet another request-specific variable component. Once you have identified the variable components, you will start building those components for each of the service-request processes from your final process list. After building those variable components, you will merge with pre-build constant components, and that will give you the final process for individual service requests.

The identification of duplicate or similar process is usually based on various components such as input data, provider, deliverables, and certain policies. For example, in most cases the request-fulfillment process for a desktop and the request-fulfillment process for a laptop could be one single process with additional selection options in input data forms, provided the delivery groups and approval policy are same. In fact, depending upon the system in which you are implementing the process, you can merge multiple processes into one process and implement the variant logic in the system that supports data-driven workflow. In that case, even if your approval policy and delivery groups are different, you can trigger different work-flow based on the data value.

Technically these are two different processes, but we are merging the implementation.

9 PROCESS IMPLEMENTATION

Process implementation has two parts:

The process tasks that are recorded and automated in a tool

Process tasks that are outside the tool

People think of tool implementation as process implementation. This would be correct if there is 100 percent automation. Most of the processes cannot be automated 100 percent and remain outside the tool. In such cases process implementation fails.

General approach

1. Each process should have a named process owner. A person can own multiple processes.

2. The process implementation should be scalable and commensurate with the size of the environment for which it is deployed.

3. The process may be automated using one or more tools; conversely, a single tool may automate multiple processes.

4. The level of process automation should depend upon the volume and magnitude of the task and cost benefit analysis.

5. Automation should not necessarily be considered to be an improvement.

6. The process may be adjusted in accordance with tool capability or limitation on the sole discretion of the process owner.

9.1 Functional Consultant for Implementation

One of the most important roles in implementation is the functional consultant. Unfortunately this role is not recognized for ITSM implementation. The prevailing roles are process consultant and tool developer. As a consequence, most of the implementations either become tool implementation or go in the loop of open-ended customization projects.

In the application management world, functional consultant is well recognized and deemed crucial for all ERP implementations. The main reason is that the application is driven by business, and none of the ERP is ever driven by technology. Unfortunately, IT service folks have never demonstrated that kind of business orientation. I emphasize the need of a functional consultant for a tool implementation for IT service management. In fact, I will rather prefer to treat it as ERP implementation.

Functional consultants bring value by combining particular ITSM process knowledge with the "know-how" of configuring the aspect of a tool that pertains to that process knowledge. Functional consultant have to understand the tools they are implementing and the set-up and configuration options available; the key skill is being able to map the requirements of the customer to the capabilities and configuration options of the tool.

The functional consultant is expected to assess and analyzes the current IT environment and generate knowledge about the current support processes to do mapping and gap analysis. The functional consultant will design the desired process for each ITSM tool module. This will define the work-flow, policy, data input, output, KPI, measurements, roles, and responsibilities. This "desired process" will be signed off by the process owner.

The process document will be translated into the functional specification that describes how the work-flow will actually function in the ITSM tool. For example, what rule should be enforced under what condition?

The functional consultant is responsible to prepare the application data for the ITSM tool with well-defined taxonomy standards. The functional consultant is sometimes also expected to prepare test scripts for testing the configured scenarios in the ITSM tool. Testing may also include unit testing, system integration testing, performance testing, user acceptance testing, or any client-specific testing.

A configuration document for ITSM tool showing all the settings and configuration has to be done by the functional consultant. An end-user manual and training is also expected from the functional consultant.

The functional consultant would need to interact with other modules' consultants; for example, the close interaction between incident management and event management will require extensive collaboration for data transfer and action triggers from the event-management system in a different system to the incident management in the ITSM tool.

Typical deliverables from functional consultant would be

1. functional specification for operation of process,

2. tool-implementation specifications,

3. templates for implementation,

4. data-point requirements for measurements,

5. procedures/work instruction,

6. use cases document, and

7. user training material.

9.2 Functional Requirements for Tools

9.2.1 Taxonomy of Process Set-Up Data

Taxonomy is a system for naming and organizing things into groups that share similar characteristics. The terms *taxonomy, cataloging, categorization,* and *classification* are often confused and used interchangeably. These are all ways of organizing information into categories.

Taxonomy is the organization of a particular set of information for a particular purpose. For any tool implementation, it helps to organize the service-management data for analysis and supporting the process improvement as well as supporting other processes outside the tool.

Taxonomy is one of the tools available for managing the information overload that people now face. While all tools may help to retrieve information and provide information about that information, each tool and its standards provide different benefits.

It is often necessary to accommodate the needs of multiple user groups or, at minimum, the different information-seeking behaviors of people in a single user group. Therefore, it is not necessary that the taxonomy applications (what the user sees) must conform to the same rules as the underlying taxonomy structure (how the data is stored in the computer).

Typical issues

After running some reports on incident management, I concluded that 9 percent of user issues are related to e-mail. When I discussed this with the service-desk manager, he told me that the correct figure is 16 percent. I showed him all the tickets in the category desktop/communication/e-mail. He informed me that there were additional categories: desktop/Outlook/PST file and exchange/account/mailbox.

I have to extract the reports from all these and add them up. I was also told that because of frequent PST file corruption, a new category has been created. Because of inconsistent taxonomy, I have a risk of losing business intelligence.

Now compare this with our day-to-day life business. I wanted to buy a pair of formal dress shoes. I entered a departmental store. I navigated the aisles by their taxonomy. I entered the "Men" section after passing the "Women," "Boys," and "Girls" sections; within that "Shoe" section followed by different aisles of sport shoes, dress shoes, and so on.

I went to another department store. There the navigation was different. There was separate "Shoe" section, and there I saw "Men's Shoes," "Women's Shoes," etc. And within Men's Shoes, I saw signs for Sports Shoes, Dress Shoes, etc.

In either case, I did not have any problem in finding the things I was looking for. What would have happened if sports shoes were in the men's section, but dress shoes in the general shoe section? I would not have found what I was looking for, and store would lose my business.

General mistakes to avoid are

1. overly vague terms;

2. lack of balance in terms;

3. gaps in coverage, sometimes severe;

4. too many top terms;

5. not enough levels ("flat" structure);

6. same term (essentially) in two places in thesaurus, but with different style;

7. two or more synonymous terms;

8. too many terms at any one level within a branch;

9. inappropriate narrower term–broad term (NT-BT) relationships;

10. term assigned entirely incorrect / inappropriate place in structure, because meaning or relationship could misunderstood or was not well-thought-out;

11. spelling errors (more common than many might think); and

12. *other* as a term or as the beginning of a term.

Hierarchical taxonomy design

Establish some general categories within the service management scope to serve tentatively as top terms. Eventually, there should be between five and twenty top terms. (Twenty is the number of terms that will fit easily in a screen display of a thesaurus hierarchy.) If it is necessary to have more, try not to have more than fifty top terms. See what terms can be grouped under an existing term. In general, it's good to go ahead and make the group narrower terms of the more general term. A term should fit completely within the category that its broader term represents. Limit the number of terms at the same level in each branch to twenty terms if practicable. If there are more than twenty terms, see if one of them could serve as a broader term for some of the narrower terms. Don't let a term become its own nephew or grandchild. In other words, a term should never appear twice in the same branch. Besides being illogical, this mistake can make future expansion problematic. It can also cause a repeating loop that impacts the reporting. Each term should be self-sufficient. Avoid using *other* as a term or as the beginning of a term. Avoid making a term reliant on a broader term to complete its sense. For example, *software* should not be a narrower term of *system* or *application*; instead, use *system software* or *application software*. The first character of each term should be consistently capitalized or lowercase, with certain exceptions. Use lowercase as much as practicable. Words with all letters capitalized are difficult to read and can be confused with acronyms.

Challenge the legacy

Why is it necessary to stick to old taxonomy that is no longer relevant? There is dramatic change in the landscape of IT service as well as in technology in the past few years, so the old way of data management will not help. Just because we have been working that way does not mean that we must continue to work the same way, especially when better ways are available. (Remember the story of monkeys in section 5.13!)

Almost every help-desk tool is designed with a CTI approach. CTI is the terminology coined by Remedy Corporation, (the leading ITSM tool provider in the industry and now a part of BMC corporation) and well understood in the industry. CTI stands for category, type, item. It is a three-tiered system for categorizing the various pieces of our infrastructure. Categorization/ classification schemes have been the keystone of all help-desk tool implementation. The quality of the CTI structure does directly affect the quality of process, as it is used for assignment/routing, reporting, searching, and even in work-flow.

This approach was originally designed in 1990s and became the de facto industry standard. In those days, the web was not pervasive; client server architecture and database-based applications were all around. The infrastructure was much simpler, hence this approach worked very well.

With the emergence of the web and service oriented architecture (SOA), IT has become extremely complex, and this CTI approach does not scale up to meet the requirements of current scenarios. With cloud computing, the categorization scheme is virtually nonviable. In other words, just like a technology becomes outdated, this scheme has become outdated. The industry needs a new approach that will serve the purpose of today's IT world. Many tool vendors have continued to follow this CTI approach. In fact, some vendors have gone even backward by expanding the outdated approach.

Then what should be the new approach?

To answer that, let us touch base on ITIL. This framework has become the de facto industry standard. This framework was also influenced by a CTI approach, up to the extent that classification and categorization was included as a process step! It was OK in the context of ITIL V2.

In ITIL V2, CMDB was deemed to be the center of the universe, around which everything revolves. This was a wrong impression, and ITIL did not really mean that. Tool vendors, for their selfish interest, promoted this notion. ITIL v3 attempted to fix this false impression. In that they made the service catalog the focal point, or the center of the ITSM universe around which everything should revolve.

In our new approach, we will combine both notions, with a clear distinction: CMDB remains the center of the internal universe, and the service catalog remains the center of the external universe.

So we would replace CTI with service and CI. In other words, if we know what service is impacted and which CI is the culprit, then we know what to do and how much important it has.

9.3   Tool Customization for Process

An organization may choose a suitable ITSM application package to innovate its ITSM processes, thereby achieving required goals. The organization then has to find an answer to the million-dollar question: whether to customize the application or use out of the box (OOB) configurations.

The OOB packages need to be evaluated on various technical attributes of process maturity and applicability to the organization. Even the best-designed or most widely used OOB configurations may meet around 70 percent of the functional requirements of an organization. Obviously, it does not make sense to acquire an ITSM application that does not meet most of the functional requirements of the organization. Very rarely are any applications (not just ITSM tools, as people often call them) implemented just out of the box. For example, Microsoft Office may be implemented out of the box, without customization. Even in this case, applications may be separately developed using Microsoft Office as a platform, especially using Excel and Word. There may also be specific regional and regulatory requirements, which may not be available out of box in most of the ITSM packages. An organization may be able to differentiate its business offerings or services through customization, such as providing enhanced reports to customers, tracking key performance indicators, or analyzing customer behavior.

The conclusion is that the customization of OOB ITSM applications is necessary to overcome functional deficiencies and meet regional and regulatory requirements. Customization may also provide the innovative edge to the enterprise. Unfortunately most ITSM vendors oversell their product and, with strong marketing techniques, make a negative impression about customization. In fact, OOB implementation of a tool usually does not serve the purpose of the users, though it definitely serves the purpose of vendors.

9.4   Process Adjustment for Tool

An organization has to ensure process fitness of the OOB ITSM application in order to minimize the effect of customization. The impact of customization is that an organization incurs additional cost toward customization of an OOB ITSM application;

the time to implement the ITSM application increases;

the customization requires maintenance support; and

whenever the OOB ITSM application is upgraded, it needs to be customized again.

Therefore, each customization should be well qualified. In some cases, when the customization is not qualified, it is recommended to alter or adjust the process backward, based on the predefined process in the tool.

9.5 Implementing Tools vs. Implementing Processes

9.5.1 The Tool Trap

In the IT service-management world, we come across many choices in the area of tools. Bigger is not necessarily better. Unfortunately, without knowledge of the real needs and tool design, most of the IT world has been going for "great" tools—going comfortably but paying more prices and most often getting worse results.

In the first chapter we talked about the artificial stupidity, and that is most pervasive in this area. OOB tool implementation is among the top evidence of attempting to solve the process problem with tools. A tool cannot solve the process problem, no matter what the vendor claim.

While tools have enormous capability to bring speed and consistency into the process execution, it is important to ensure that there is no blind dependency on the tool. People talk about human errors and human failures, but tools are also liable to fail. Therefore, there must be some recourse for the situation where tools fail, and quite possibly the recourse could be manual. For example, if you are running a retail business, and your POS system fails, then you will not stop your business; you will do the manual operation at the counter using a calculator or even pen and paper. Your ability will be limited, but it will not be zero. However, if the same thing happens at Walmart, the manager will open another counter where the POS is working. The important point is the recourse to a tool failure could be manual or another backup tool. In operations, it is not possible to have backup tool for everything; therefore, people must be trained to do things manually. Improper automation without alternate recourse can make a tool failure even messier.

We see lot of tools everywhere, not only in IT but beyond, in all aspects of our daily life. When I visit the Home Depot tool section, I see mind-boggling choices of tools, many of them with overlapping functionality. Even though I believe they are the right tool for many kinds of work in my home, I still do not buy. More than 90 percent of my home-maintenance work is done by a limited tool set that includes a screwdriver set, a drilling machine with drill bits, a hammer, a handsaw, etc. If I have any need beyond this, I would rather call a professional handyman and get that 10 percent home-maintenance work done rather than buy a sophisticated tool and get amused about how to use it appropriately. Also, it is more likely that I will do bad work, even though I am using good tool. I see a similar situation in the IT world. Organizations buy sophisticated tools sold by the promise of a vendor of what it can do, but they forget that

1. they already have some tool with overlapping functionality;

2. buying the tool is different from using the tool;

3. using the tool is different from bringing the desired outcome from that tool; and

4. the existing tool, if appropriately used, can give cost-effective results.

Of course, organizations might have some sophisticated requirement, but it is much better to hire a professional to deal with that requirement rather than buying that sophisticated tool.

9.5.2 Right Implementation

Tools cannot solve process problems. Tool implementation is not a purpose by itself. It is a means to achieve the goals established by process. A successful tool implementation will focus on process and then use the tool capability to serve the process and to enable or improve the outcome.

A tool does not usually automate the complete process. Some parts of the process always remain outside the tool. For example, once you submit an emergency RFC, the work-flow might take you to the closure, but who, under what condition, submits emergency RFC is the role that comes before the tool, and that is addressed in process. So when you implement a tool, you actually automate some work-flow, you enable some data collection for measurement, and you might even have implemented certain rules, but you still did not implement a complete process.

Why are OOB implementations a flawed implementation of process? Because they implement only the work-flow—a part of process—and keep you under the illusion that the process is implemented. In fact, OOB implementation is a faulty concept propagated by tool vendors to serve their purposes. You very well know that even a laptop/desktop operating system like Windows 7 cannot be used out of the box and you need to create a specific image for your organization to use it within the organization. How an enterprise grade ITSM application can be used out of the box?

So you need to use the tools as the enabling product and plan for the right implementation.

A right implementation of process makes the right choice between policy enforcement and judicious application of guidelines. While policies are made to be enforced, not every policy *can* be enforced, and on many occasions guidelines and their judicious use are more effective. In many worthy situations, we make exception and make over-deliveries. Technically over-delivery is a leakage of revenue, but it is also a very good tool to create good perception. Occasional over-delivery is good, but frequent over-delivery is counterproductive.

Right implementation also leads to process adoption. A process is good up to the extent it is adopted. In process maintenance, compliance measurement tells you how effectively a process is adopted.

Right implementation will give adequate emphasis on role-mapping—that is, assigning the right role to the right person. Even the best process will fail if the roles designed in the process are not mapped to the right person.

Each role has obligations. Each process is designed to serve someone internally or externally. Therefore, a good result will demand that each role-player discharge his or her duty faithfully. In several customer-facing processes, the customer has also some role to play and should be bound by the obligation of that role. For example, in incident-management process, anyone in the role of incident-reporter customer is obligated to provide symptom description and user experience data including screen shots. If he or she does not do this duty, the good result may not come. So if customers are getting bad service, he or she may be responsible. In general it is not completely wrong to say, "A customer gets the level of service that he or she deserves."

Finally, in right implementation, there is a great deal of organization change management, but I do not intend to cover that aspect in this book.

9.5.3 Misuse/Wrong Use of Tools

Tools are often designed to support the process but most often to circumvent the processes. I will site two most prominent examples:

Patch management: Several vendors are marketing patch-management tools as a solution rather than a tool. So-called automated solution is a pack of feature and functions that the tool can do, and vendors encourage you to use those and indirectly contribute circumvention of the process, so you have a tool that will automatically download the patch and automatically deploy as well. The critical controls that are usually part of the process are forgotten here. A right approach to use the tool will be as follows:

1. A patch will always be under change control; that means there must be an RFC for patch deployment.

2. The RFC must go through the approval process.

3. A well-defined change-control process will automatically demand the verification of patch and of testing.

4. After verification and satisfactory testing results, RFC is approved then the deployment process will be triggered using the tool. The deployment part will be invariably automated; however, the trigger can be manual, or an orchestration tool can trigger the deployment process upon approval of RFC.

5. Some of the integration considerations are that the job can be created in the tool, and that can trigger the RFC in ITSM tool, and the approval status in ITSM tool can run the job in patch-management tool.

From the above steps, it is clear that the steps 1 through 3 are the process parts and will remain outside the patch-management tool.

CMDB updating through discovery tools: It is very common practice to deploy a Discovery tool and integrate with CMDB. This is yet another example of circumventing the change-management process. For example, a person makes some unauthorized change without a RFC. Because of automation, this will be detected, and CMDB will be updated. Unauthorized modification has thus become a valid record in CMDB. Where are the controls?

The correct method would be as follows:

1. There will be a RFC, which will go through proper controls and approval processes.

2. Upon the completion of the RFC, a CMDB update should be triggered.

3. This trigger should fetch the correct data and update the CMDB.

4. This data-fetching should not be for the entire record, but be corresponding to the RFC only.

5. Most often a handful of CI records will be modified, and it can be manually updated within ten minutes on the completion of RFC.

The problem is that people do not want to do the housekeeping job as a part of change management, and they are obsessed with automation. The proper use of discovery tool is in the two areas:

At the beginning of establishing a CMDB baseline discovery tool, it will be extremely useful to fetch the data and be one of the important data sources for creating a CMDB baseline.

It will not be the only data source, as a tool cannot discover all attributes; for example, physical location of the CI or the service owner.

Another important use of the discovery tool is in the audit process of configuration control. That means that the discovery tool will discover actual data matches with the CMDB record and match the deviation with RFC. In fact, it is also a tool to detect unauthorized changes.

9.5.4 Implementation Pitfalls

Resource planning: Short-term resource requirements

During the implementation and the initial operation of new processes, the resource requirements go up. Support staff is common among all the processes. The same staff will now be doing some of the capacity management, availability management, and problem-management activities. This will seem to be an extra work, but the consequence of this work will be induced incidents, increased quality, increased service levels, and reduction of crisis situations. These benefits will be realized over a period of time. However, short-term increments may add to the workload and/or have additional resource requirements, so it will be a trade-off.

Expecting major benefits too quickly

There will be some quick wins, but the major benefits will start coming over a period of time. In fact, during the initial period, the services may even decline, or conflicts may surface. For example, the enforcement of certain discipline may seem to be bureaucratic and counterproductive; however, long-term benefits must be kept in mind.

Loss of impetus

It is a huge effort to implement all ITIL processes—taking most organizations three years or more for all the phases—and maintain the momentum. This is a long time to maintain momentum, but it is like taking a course of antibiotics when you are ill. After a few doses, you feel better. But if you fail to complete the whole course of the prescription, you will soon be back to square one—feeling ill again.

Synchronization of individual projects

It is rare that you might be pursuing one project at any given point of time. Many projects are interrelated and must be synchronized. For example, you spend a lot of time and energy to reengineer a server provisioning process and automate it. By the time it is ready, you realized that a virtualization project is also finished that eliminated the need of physical server provisioning!

Not creating work instructions

Work instructions should be written, published, and continually reviewed with operational staff. This has been described in section 4.1 about work instructions.

Not assigning process owners

A process owner should be assigned to each of the ITIL processes that cross functional silos. The process owner should concentrate on the structure and flow of the process, without having to focus on staffing and other departmental issues. A process owner's job is to carefully monitor and manage the assigned processes, so that it can be continually improved.

Do not get overambitious for absolute perfection: it is pragmatic to accept that good enough is OK; that a few gaps can be lived with; that the world functions on imperfect information; that pragmatic considerations mean we have to stop at some point; and that business is all about taking considered risks over known exposures and prioritizing to make best use of limited resources.

Allowing departmental demarcation

Processes cross more than one department, often causing conflict among departments, especially where department boundaries are rigid, and ownership is important. All departments need to understand that ITIL is a joint venture, and success comes from all working together; that is, the power of unity.

Communication

Continuous communication is the key for a successful rollout of the processes. Everyone will be impacted. In the communication, include what is going to happen, when it will happen, what is expected from individuals, and what individuals will get out of it.

- Involve IT staff and customers as well

- Do active selling / awareness

- Make sure people know what is going to happen

- Make sure people understand *why* it happens

- Don't leave them in the dark; make them smart

9.5.5 Deficiency in implementation

When we say we implemented a process in the tools then we mean that we to put the tool into effect according to the defined process and functional requirements. So, upon implementation of the tool, the expected outcome is that the tool (or you can say ITSM application) is working, and that means all the codes are running as written. But is that the purpose? What you really want is that the process is producing the desired result. When tool is implemented then exe file or dll file running will not necessarily produce the desired result of the process

Here is the problem. There is a huge difference between the tool is running and process is running or process is delivering the desired outcome. Implementation must go beyond the process workshop, creating functional requirements, customizing/configuring tools, performing UAT, conduction trainings and so on. The right implementation will go beyond that and following are a few such points.

Role mapping

Every process defines one or more roles for its operation. During the implementation, you must identify the individuals and ensure that all the roles defined in the process are assigned. It is very important to map the role to the right person. The person, to whom the role is mapped, is trained to perform that role. In some cases, empowerment may also be required to perform the role. Also, the accountability and the responsibility of the role should roll up to a live person. When you automate the tasks, for example escalation email notification, the tool is performing the task but that does not mean that the Incident manager is not accountable for communication. The Incident manager is said to be using the tool for the job but the communication tasks are still under his or her role.

Many cracks in the processes are actually the result of missing role mapping or the wrong role mapping.

Compatibility of functional organization

You may define the role and map the roles appropriately but is your organization is functionally designed to support those roles? One very common example is the change manager and the change control board in most of the organization exists on paper and also mapped to the individuals but change manager is not adequately empowered and the change control board does not have charter.

Service desk is defined as the single point of contact but lacks the control. End users who have issues and have opened ticket and yelling at service desk but the resolution actions are with some other group and that group would not be influenced by service desk priorities.

Capacity management process and availability management process is very likely to fail in the absence of dedication function like capacity management and availability management.

So, it is not only the matter of to whom the role is mapped but also how that person is mapped in the organization structure.

Organization Change management

Process change will bring in the change in the way of working and it is a separate and specialized subject. Resistance to a change is very natural. IT organization will also need a focused approach on this to ensure that the processes are institutionalized and adopted.

10 PROCESS MAINTENANCE

10.1 What Is Process Maintenance?

In section 3.3.2 we compared process maintenance with software mainte-nance. Process maintenance deals with the activities of keeping the process in usable condition. That means maintaining the efficiency and effectiveness of the process. Process maintenance makes the service quality sustainable.

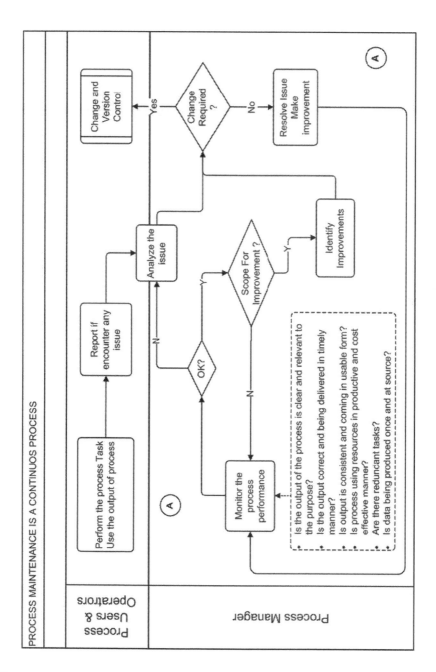

Figure 29: Process maintenance

Generally process maintenance tasks are classified into corrective, adaptive, perfective, and preventive categories.

10.1.1 Corrective tasks

Corrections relate to the diagnosis, localization, and actual fixing of errors. Debugging and testing relate intimately to this class. During the operation some bug might be reported. The process is broken, patchy, or it is delivering faulty results. The process manager must take two actions:

provide a work-around

remove the bug by process modification

For example, in a change-management process, a rule was enforced in the tool to relate a change request (CR) to a CI at the time of submission, but the CMDB was not updated. As a result, even though the server existed in production environment, the CR could not be submitted. Relating a CI to CR is mandatory at the time of processing it; now it is mandatory to relate CI to an incident ticket also.

10.1.2 Adaptive Tasks

Adaptive tasks deal with interfacing existing processes to changing environments. For example, an event-management process was used by one group for server events but is now applied on application events also. Incident management was providing input to the problem management but now is providing the input to availability management also.

10.1.3 Perfective Tasks

Additions, enhancements, and modifications are made to the code based on (generally often) changing user needs. Because of inevitable changes in business situations, processes needs upgrading. For example, a cost-cutting measure required two approvals for a service-request process of a new BlackBerry account. Originally it required one approval. Repetitive tasks like a Windows security patch update require approval from a computing services manager only rather than the complete CAB.

10.1.4 Preventive Maintenance

Preventive maintenance aims for the enhancement of future maintainability of the process. For example, a measurement built into the process will require continuous maintenance because of an ad hoc reporting requirement.

10.1.5 Process Maintenance Examples

Process maintenance example 1

We implemented an access-management process where all the steps were very well defined. If a requestor is asking for an access to a server, an approval will be required from the owner of the server. The operation of this process requires a database that will provide the owner's name against each server. At the time of implementing this process, the availability of this database was assured (it was part of a CMDB). The process was running very well till one owner of a server, when access to the server was granted without his approval, escalated the incident to be a process breakdown. The investigation revealed that the approval was indeed obtained before granting the access. However, the approval of another person was obtained. Further investigation revealed that the approver was also listed as the owner of the same server, so it was not even a wrong approval. This is a typical example of a process bug, where the designer does not envisage that a server can have multiple owners in exceptional cases. This situation warranted enhancement in the existing process to add the policy of "anyone or all" approval. This example illustrates that even if the process is adequate at the time of implementation, it will not remain adequate in the future.

Process maintenance example 2

We implemented a service-request-management as well as an incident-management process to distinctively deal with both kinds of requests. There was a strict policy that service requests can be submitted only via web, while incidents will be accepted via phone and e-mail as well as the web. One day a customer reported an incident: his network drive was abnormally slow. This was registered as an incident. Investigation of this incident revealed that the customer's network drive was mapped in the storage that physically existed in a different geography. Because of the WAN speed, the slower performance was normal and expected. When the explanation was provided to the customer, he asked to relocate his network drive to the same physical location where he actually was working. The service-desk agent asked him to submit a service request, because such request was published in a standard service request catalog on the web. The policy was cited that service requests cannot be accepted by phone or e-mail. The customer insisted on our delivering the service under the same incident, because the network drives should have been created at the physical location where he was working.

The situation was resolved amicably with a variety of arguments in support of either party:

The original service request to create a network drive was incorrectly executed; instead of location A, the drive was created in location B.

If this was incorrectly executed, then the customer has the right to rework without any additional ticket.

The original SR ticket was closed, so rework could not be done under the same ticket. (The customer has five business days to confirm the correct work, after which the ticket is closed).

The customer has no mechanism to check the correctness of the location of the drive.

The service desk has no mechanism to register a service request via phone.

This looks like a complex situation, but here comes the discretionary power of the service desk agent: As we said earlier there are certain guidelines and certain policies. While the service-desk agent complied with the policy, within the situation he also used guidelines to satisfy the customer.

10.1.6 Monitoring

Process monitoring is the observation and checking done to measure the satisfactory performance of the process. Satisfactory performance is determined during process design and often stems from the results of process benchmarking.

In addition, processes can be monitored over a long periods of time to see how they perform over several process instances. When actual results are compared to targets, the gap between the two becomes data that process owners and other stakeholders use to take corrective action.

Process monitoring requires not just performance measurement but feedback systems that enable the measurement data to reach the stakeholders. The process performance will be measured by the KPIs defined for each process.

Performance monitoring parameters examples

1. Quality of information recorded in the incident ticket work log

2. Analyzing CR to ensure observe information required by approvers for evaluation, but not provided by change requestors initially, leading to increased total turnaround time

3. Customer satisfaction (CSAT) scores and comments

4. Monthly SLA reports

5. Status trending reports for CRs

10.1.7 Monitoring Method/Tasks and Criteria

Processes will normally be automated in work-flow tool, but some part will be manual. The process manager will evaluate this criteria reactively when some issue has been reported or some SLA breach investigation has lead the issue in the process or proactively picked up tickets by random sampling.

10.2 Process Improvement

10.2.1 Process Ineffectiveness Indicators

In order for a process to be effective, all the sub processes need to be effective. For an effective service-management process such as incident or problem management, the IT process within it is should also be effective; that is, technical work is in compliance with product/technology best practice. The following symptoms are a no-brainer conclusion for ineffective processes:

1. Unacceptable outcome

2. Customer complaints

3. Backlog of work

4. Redoing the completed work

5. Rejected output

6. Late output

7. Incomplete output

Every consequence of a bad or an ineffective process converges into customer dissatisfaction. People can argue that the process is good, but one of the role players did not perform the task correctly. Well, I can counter-argue that the process was not implemented correctly, as during the implementation we failed to assign the right role to the right person and probably also did not conduct training to do the task correctly. In other words, if we know that customers are dissatisfied, then we should conclude that one or more processes are not working correctly or not implemented correctly. This conclusion is merely a symptom, and you need to investigate with data and make a correct conclusion. I have come across many organizations that know the symptom but end up giving a wrong diagnosis; for example, most people often think that the service desk is accountable for customer satisfaction. That is like blaming the ticket-booking agent for bad airline service!

10.2.2 Process Improvement Areas

The key area of process improvement includes the following:

Simplification could be in the way of doing the task or simplifying the data entry. For example, in change management you need to enter a variety of controlled data, such as test plan, back-out plan, or risk analysis. A structured data entry approach can greatly simplify this activity.

Hardening is to make it difficult to take wrong steps. This is also associated with the robustness of the process. One common example is not to allow submission of emergency change requests unless until certain qualifying parameters are met.

Elimination of bureaucracy implies the elimination of redundant tasks. I have often seen a high degree of bureaucracy in change-management process, especially the controls built around approvals. Very often, "for your approval" can be replaced with "for your information."

Elimination of duplicity—duplicity may not only be inefficient but also error-prone, as well as irritating to the customer. I have often seen that certain kinds of data or information is collected from the customer during the initial stage in a service-request process, and the same data is solicited again at a later stage in the process.

Standardizing the activity—if all the actors in the process are doing the same task in the same manner, it will eliminate the errors due to variations in the task and methods.

Automation of routine tasks is a very common method of improvement but can be risky if unqualified tasks are automated. You should be in control of automation.

Cycle time reduction—the overall duration of process can be optimized by reducing the idle-state period.

10.3 Process Assessment

Often the most challenging parts of any process-improvement effort is in knowing where to begin. Process maturity assessment is designed as a starting point for embarking on the journey of IT service and process improvements. As an IT organization's ability to deliver quality IT services to its business customers is directly related to its overall organizational and process maturity, service is designed to evaluate key operational and process activities and provide a snapshot of maturity.

While in many organizations no processes have been formally implemented, many of the activities related to processes would exist. A process-maturity assessment exercise will help to determine the degree to which the process activities exist, the relative maturity of those processes, as well as create a baseline for process improvement. The following diagram depicts the assessment method:

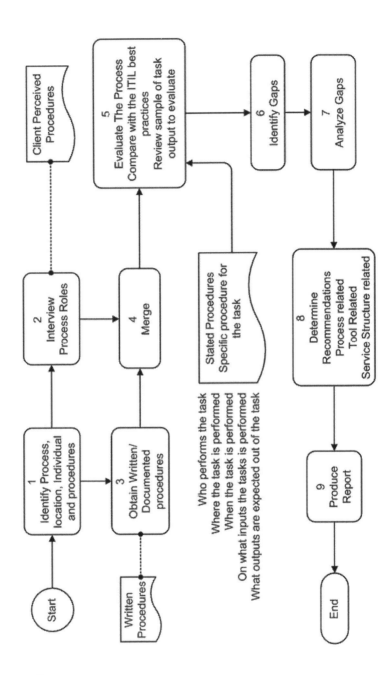

Figure 30: Process assessment

Evaluation for maturity is based on the following questions:

1. Is the recommended best practice followed? (intent of best practice met)

2. If not, is there any compensating practice for the gap?

3. Is the output of the process clear and relevant to the purpose?

4. Is the output correct and being delivered in timely manner?

5. Is the output consistent and coming in usable form?

6. Is the process using resources in a productive and cost-effective manner?

7. Are there redundant tasks?

8. Is data being produced only once and at the source?

10.4 Soft Maintenance of Processes

You may have designed the processes very well; you have implemented them very well and taken care of organization change-management also. You may be doing good maintenance of processes, but you may find that something is still not working as desired. In other words, the process may be working as designed, but results may not be coming as desired. This is where the soft-maintenance aspect of process comes into the picture.

In the section 5.13.1, "Why Processes Fail," we established that lack of faith in the process is one of the reasons that people do not follow a process; hence the process breaks. If people do not believe that a thing will work, they will not follow through and may unknowingly make it *not* work (thereby fulfilling their prejudiced belief). Thus the soft maintenance becomes a crucial part of process management. This deals with the job of creating faith in the processes. It is matters of making people believe that the process exists and the process is right.

Process exists

Process exists is another statement that the process is complete. When you design and implement a process, it must be complete. Completeness is another aspect of process. As we have established earlier, the work-flow is a small part of the process, and a complete process includes policies as well. Nonexistence of policies within processes to deal with circumstances arising during process execution is in fact related to the completeness of the process, but this absence of policy gives an illusion that process does not exist to deal with the present circumstance. The soft maintenance is not responsible for designing processes but takes care to continually market them to provide assurance to the users that the process exists, thus motivating people to use the process.

Process is right

People can never have faith in broken processes or processes that are ineffective (people may live with inefficient processes but not ineffective processes). While hard maintenance will address the issue of ineffectiveness, soft maintenance will still have a public relation responsibility to maintain customer faith.

It is the primary responsibility of the process owner to ensure that people have faith and trust in his process. It is like the brand image of the product. It is an irony that people demonstrate more faith in tools rather than in processes. This is in fact the result of vendors' marketing the product. Process owners should learn those marketing points and use those points to supplement their own marketing of the processes.

10.5 Vicious Circle of Process Improvement

Good things cost money. Process improvements require appreciable efforts. Although we described the methods and approach for the improvement, you must be aware of a typical vicious circle that you encounter in every organization. I have depicted the circle in the picture in the diagram below:

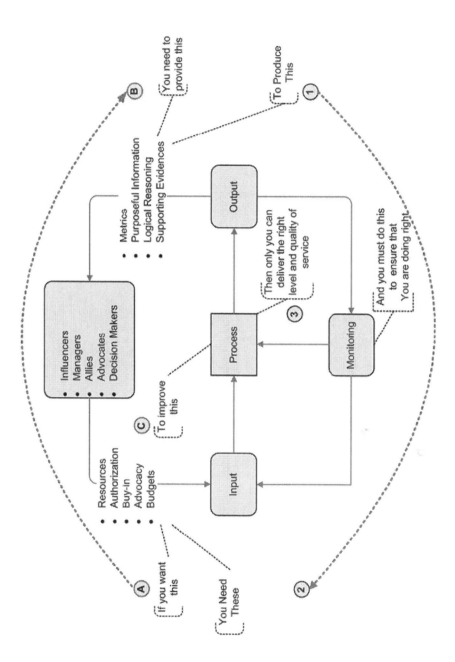

Figure 31: Vicious circle of process improvement

You want several things to make process improvement, such as resources, authorization to change, buy-in to do the right things, advocacy to make your work streamlined, and of course the budgets.

In order to obtain all the above, you will need metrics: a lot of metrics about process KPIs and purposeful information with logical reasoning and supporting evidences from the metrics.

However, many times the process needs improvement only for capturing the right metric, so you need to implement improvement to justify improvement!

This is a vicious circle and can be broken bit by bit. Once you get a point of entry, you will be able to move around easily in the continual loop of improvement. The assessment should find out quick wins for process improvement, also from the point of view of process management.

11 PROCESS INTEGRATION

Process integration is a technique of attaining close and seamless coordination and interaction of processes. It is a connection of two or more processes in harmony and a logical manner, as if the tasks within the process were connected in logical manner. By virtue of integration, processes can share data and even actions with each other. Integrated processes are significantly more effective than the sum of individual processes in isolation.

11.1 Basic Concept

Process Integration is one of the key techniques to unify the effect and outcome of multiple processes. . Process can share the data and even actions with each other. Integrated Processes are significantly more effective than sum of individual process in isolation.

I am presenting a process-integration framework based on the process relationship defined in ITIL. The driving theme of the framework is as follows:

Each process is obligated to deliver some input (trigger or data) to another process. For example, in many conditions, if an incident is resolved with a work-around, a problem-management process ought to be triggered. Incident management is obligated to provide this trigger along with the data of symptom, diagnosis, and observation about the incident.

This process has a right to expect some input from other processes to be effective. For example, the capacity-management process must receive utilization data from the event-management process.

Here are the typical integration examples about how the processes give triggers and data to each other.

11.1.1 Elements of Process Integration

There are three fundamental elements of process integration:

Event is the moment of occurrence in the process lifecycle that may be captured in an element of time. Many events do occur during the run time of a process. Some of them will initiate the action of integration. For example, resolution of an incident is the event that is captured in the run-time operation of an incident-management process and could trigger a problem-management process.

Data that is produced during the run-time of a process could be structured or unstructured. During the integration, relevant data is provided to another process. The format of the data required by a process may be different than the format required by the receiving process. The data transformation to the right format is considered while integrating the process. Data integration ensures that information in multiple processes is kept consistent as well as that data is reused.

Condition dictates the executions of defined integration actions (usually by triggering another event or transferring data).

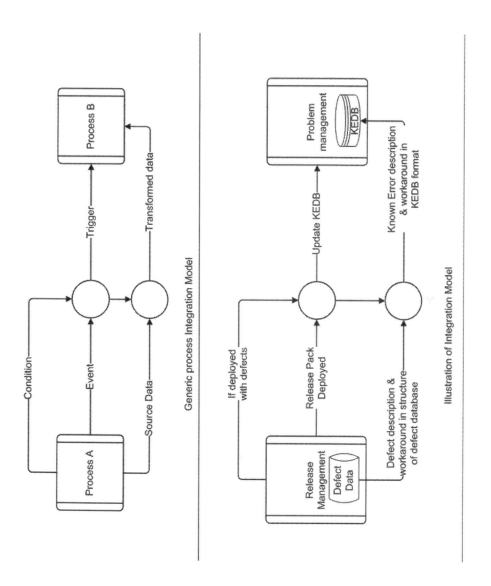

Figure 32: process integration model

11.1.2 Mechanism of Process Integration

There are three broad mechanisms to integrate processes—manual, semiauto-mated, and fully automated. Most environments involve a combination of first two types. The third type—fully automated—is rarely possible, because human intervention is an integral part of service delivery and service support. Although some sub processes or individual processes can be fully automated, such as event management and SOP-based run books—and even limited integration across individual processes can be automated—the integration automation across mul-tiple processes is not yet found to be feasible, because invariably there will be some guideline in a process that will require a judicious decision from a person.

Manual process integration

Manual process integration implies actors to act as the interfaces between pro-cesses and enable the integration between them. This form of process integra-tion is very common. In the example in section 10.1.1, a person (say, a release manager) will send an e-mail to another person (say, a problem manager) stating the business reasons for the business's demanding to go live: despite defects that are not deemed to be showstoppers, the benefits of time-to-market prevails. In this e-mail the release manager will attach an Excel file of these defects and the remedial measures. Upon receipt of this e-mail, the problem manager will map the appropriate fields of the Excel file to the KEDB structure and upload the file.

This form of integration requires very little technology investment. It becomes more complex, however, when the service environment becomes more com-plex, and it can lead to inaccuracies in data and events. As the amount and complexity of events, data, and conditions increase, or as the number of pro-cesses increases, you will require more and more people to maintain such an environment. An environment that relies heavily on manual integration is generally very inefficient and does not grow as easily as environments that use more automated techniques.

Although the advantage is that existing low-technology environments require little change, the disadvantages are higher people costs, scalability, and the prevalence of human error.

Semiautomated process integration

Semiautomated process integration combines actors' actions with some level of automation. A person may be involved in an area where an automated solution is not feasible or is difficult or expensive to implement. More often it could be that the policy or guideline implementation cannot be encoded in a tool algorithm and thus requires a person to make decisions. In this example, an event may automatically trigger an e-mail notification and automatically attach the defect list, but the task of transforming data and uploading could be manual.

Semiautomated process integration usually requires more technology investment, but once that investment is made, you can often reduce the workload on people operating the process. Reducing human involvement in this manner usually reduces costs and increases reliability.

This gives the advantage of lower labor costs, better scales, fewer human errors, and faster processing but gives the disadvantage of higher technology costs to implement and being subject to design-time and run-time errors.

Fully automated process integration

Fully automated process integration removes people from all three elements of process integration (event, data, and condition) entirely, although it does not eliminate the need for maintenance. This type of integration consists of process communicating through a series of sets of data and events bidirectionally. In the above example, defective database fields and KEDB fields will be mapped, and data will be transformed on the fly.

Although fully automated process integration removes the dependency on people, such integration can be more expensive to implement and may not be practical for multiple process integration across multiple support groups. As stated earlier, the integration of full automation across multiple processes is not yet found to be feasible, because invariably there will be some guideline in process that will require a judicious decision from a person.

Fully automated process integration brings in the advantage of lowest process operation costs, elimination of human error at run time, and faster task execution. On the other hand, disadvantages are the high costs to implement the relevant technology, and that a fully automated process is prone to design errors.

11.1.3 Making Process Integration Scalable

An important part of making process integration scalable is to increase the number of automated steps and reduce the number of human steps. This can be done by creating clear and crisp policies that are not subject to interpretation within the processes and that also define interfaces between processes with a clear definition of the three elements of integration.

The scalability does not stop imply simple automation. You should think of the number of interdependent processes and how integration occurs between them. There are two models: point-to-point and integration-hub.

Point-to-point model

The point-to-point model describes a decentralized structure in which each process communicates directly with the other process. This type of integration is most appropriate for transactional processes.

The number of interfaces required for point-to-point integration increases rapidly as indicated in the diagram below—you require three interfaces for three processes, but, if you increase two more processes, the interface count increases by seven.

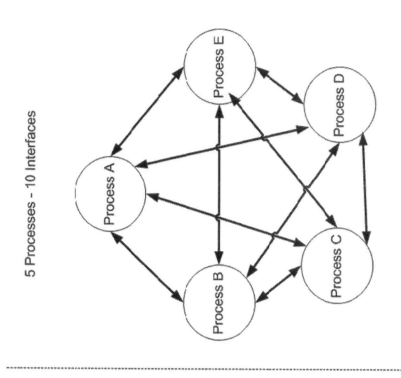

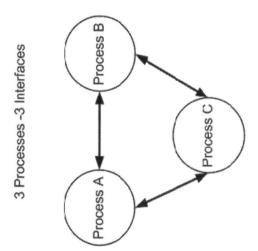

Figure 33:Point to point integration

In a point-to-point integration environment, interfaces between the processes are often defined on a needs basis, and this leads to inconsistency. Every change makes the environment more complex and increases the cost of maintenance.

The integration-hub model

In this model, integration among the processes happens via a common hub. Each process needs one interface and a connection to the integration hub. The main advantage of an integration hub environment is scalability.

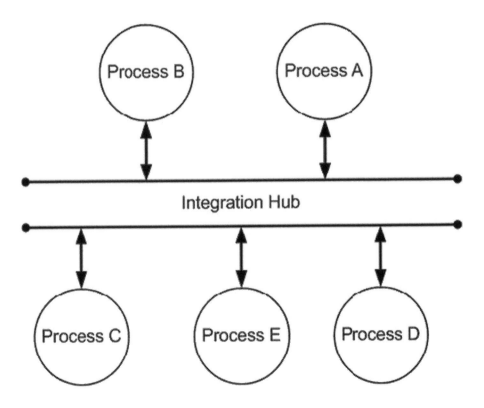

Figure 34: Integration hub

The integration-hub model is significantly more scalable for integration environments with many processes. Typically in an organization there are multiple processes because of many different vendors' outsourcing situations. You simply cannot create individual interfaces for every point of interaction. Instead, the solution is to create a process integration environment that allows all your processes to communicate in a logical, predefined way. One very common and first-level need is to integrate the processes' data for a common view of service outcomes.

What is the right model?

As you analyze the service environment, you will need to determine whether a point-to-point model, an integration-hub model, or a combination of the two is most appropriate. Realistically, the decision you make will be based on cost and value. In many cases, process integration involves a combination of both models, using point-to-point initially, and then moving to the use of one or more integration hubs as complexity increases and when there are clear business benefits to doing so. Following is my general recommendation:

1. Start with transaction-based processes.

2. Use point-to-point integration between five key operational processes.

3. Consider SLA data integration a priority, as "single view of end-to-end service" is the prime business driver.

Leverage the CMDB and service portfolio as the two data hubs within the integration.

11.1.4 Origination of Integration

Most of the IT processes originate from three sources. In fact, these are the only three sources from where any process starts.

A configuration item: all the configuration items will be monitored under an event-management process or a batch-job-monitoring process. These are the source of events.

End users: the end users will trigger either an incident-management process or an IMAC process.

Business: the business will trigger a project request, which will eventually trigger a release-management process.

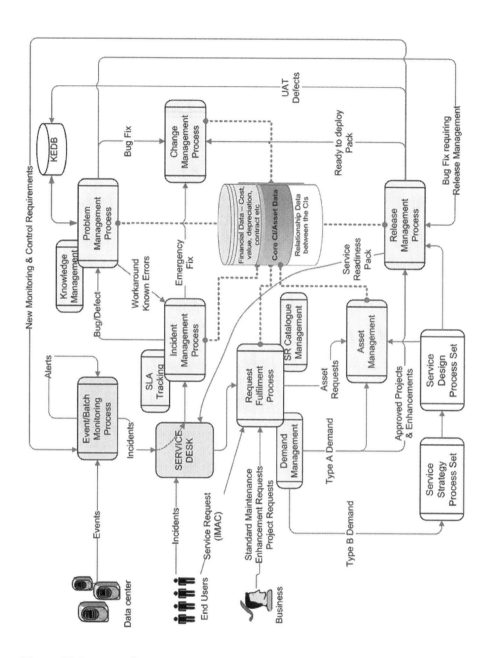

Figure 35: Integrated processes in action

Process integration

Event management will deal with all the events and control responses on all events. This includes events coming from batch-job monitoring. When a control response within event management does not resolve an error condition, it will trigger an incident-management process. At this point the data supplied by event management to incident management will include CI information and incident description.

The end user will trigger an incident by reporting some issue to the service desk by multiple methods. It is quite possible that an incident reported by the end user has already been reported by an event-management process.

The end user will also trigger a service-request process.

Businesspeople will trigger project request or service-modification requests. That will eventually trigger multiple processes, primarily release management. However, before release management are service-design processes. Businesspeople will have demands that can change the portfolio, and that will trigger service strategy and design processes that will eventually come in production through release management.

An incident may turn out to be a bug or defect. In that case it will trigger a problem-management process. At this time incident management will supply its diagnosis data to problem management along with various other data about categorization and classification.

When problem management is triggered, it will feed back the authorized workaround to incident management for fixing the incident. Eventually, problem management will identify the root cause (known error) and update the KEDB. This KEDB will be supplying all the data to the incident-management process till the time the root cause is fixed.

After supplying the work-around and KEDB to incident management, problem management will also trigger a change-management or release-management process. When change management has implemented the change, it will update KEDB and send that particular record in an active state, because the known error has been eliminated.

A release-management process will trigger a change-management process when the deployment pack is ready.

Release management will also trigger event management to prepare for monitoring and control of new services.

Release management will also trigger service readiness data for incident management.

It is not unusual that release packs are less than perfect, and there are known bugs. There may be a business compulsion to deploy these packs, because those bugs are not showstoppers. At this point release management will supply the data to KEDB, so that the incident-management process is ready to deal with those defects.

Incident management may bypass problem management and directly trigger a change-management process for emergency fixes.

CMDB will be a common port for data exchange among all the processes.

We can expand this simplistic view further and name each process interface and describe it. In the diagram below, the named connection defines the input and output interface between the processes. Each process creates and maintains the data during its operation, which can be shared with other processes. There are varieties of databases. Each database is owned and managed by at least one process.

Following is the relationship between database and process:

The event-transaction database is owned and managed by event-management process and used primarily by capacity management and availability management.

A CMIS—capacity management information system—is structured and unstructured data that is owned, managed, and used by capacity management and service-level management.

An AMIS—availability management information system—is owned and managed by availability management and used by availability management and service-level management.

The service-transaction database includes the ticket database for incident, problem, change, and request and is managed and owned by the set of interconnected processes—incident, problem, change, and request—and used by the service-level management process, availability management, and capacity management.

DSL is extension of CMDB and used by the release-management process as well as the request-management process.

The service portfolio is managed by service-portfolio management, and a part of it is a service catalog that is owned and managed by service-catalog management. A service portfolio is used by service-level management.

The security-management information system is the encompassing system across all the processes and is owned by security-management process and enforced on all the processes. Service knowledge management system (SKMS) is the global database that all the processes contribute to.

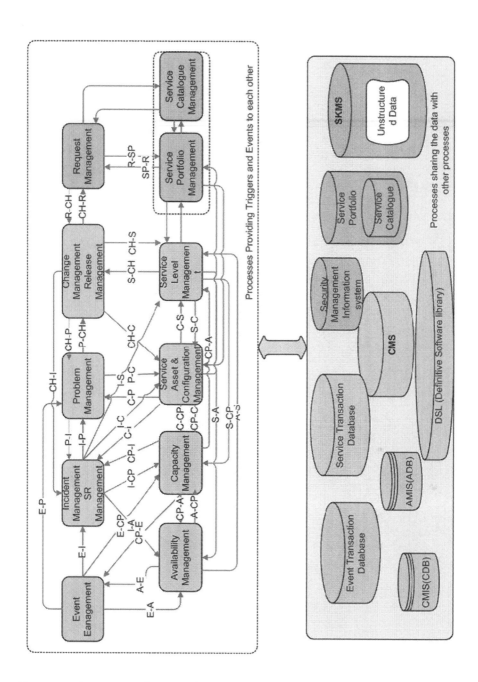

Figure 36: Integration framework

The following table provides descriptions of process interfaces,

Interface	Description
E-I	When control response within event management does not resolve an error condition, it will trigger an incident-management process. At this point the data supplied by event management to incident management will include CI information and incident description.
E-A	The event-management process detects the non-availability at source and provides the data to the availability-management process.
A-E	Availability management dictates the availability monitoring requirement to the event-management process.
E-P	The event-management process provides the patterns of events, warnings, and error conditions to enable problem management to effect proactive problem elimination.
E-CP	Certain events may decline the performance of service or breach the capacity threshold. EM process will supply the capacity-usage data to capacity-management process.
CP-E	Capacity management dictates the performance-monitoring requirement and usage threshold limits to the event-management process.
I-P	Incident management may trigger problem management under certain conditions such as critical incident resolved by work-around and repeat incidents.
I-CP	Incident management reports capacity-related incidents to capacity management. This includes performance decline and surge in demand. Such data will help capacity management improve.
C-E, C-I, C-P, C-CH C-R, C-A, C-CP, C-S C-SP, C-SC	The configuration-management database (CMDB), under the control of the configuration-management process, is the data provider to all the processes. It is also a port of exchange or a bridge to connect indirectly. For example, an incident related to a CI may find its connection to the problem linked to the same CI and/or a change linked to the same CI. CMDB is also holds the service portfolio as well as the service catalog (if service is defined as CI).

Interface	Description
I-CH	An incident may trigger emergency change.
I-S	An incident provides the SLA achievement report about incident SLAs, such as response time and resolution time.
S-I	The service-level management process dictates the targets and standards of the service levels. It also provides the OLA.
P-I	The problem-management process is obligated to provide KEDB and work-around to incident management. In case incident management has produced the work-around on its own, it should be validated by problem management.
P-CH	Problem management will identify known errors and trigger a change-management process by creating an RFC.
CH-P	Change management will provide the info on the successful RFC implementation that was triggered by problem management, so that problem management retires the corresponding KEDB record.
S-CH	The SLM process will dictate the change policies, such as change freeze period and duration of maintenance windows for planned changes.
CH-S	Details of approved changes should be communicated to service-level management to evaluate the impact of change on agreed service levels.
R-CH	Release management provides status updates on its progress to change management.
CH-R	Change management provides authorization and approval to release management.
A-S	Availability management provides data (in terms of reports, trend analysis, etc.) on existing availability of service components. It also provides details of critical service components and single points of failure, which is used to evaluate SLAs/OLAs.

Interface	Description
A-CP	Availability management provides availability requirements for to ensure that adequate capacity is provisioned for all service components, and there is no service unavailability due to lack of capacity.
CP-S	Capacity management obtains the performance-related SLA from SLM process and provides the data of available capacity and forecasting about required capacity.
S-CP	SLM dictates the performance-related SLA to be achieved to capacity management.
S-A	SLM dictates the availability-related SLA to be achieved to availability management.
R-SP	Request management may encounter some of the demands that have direct impact on the portfolio; such demands will be passed on to portfolio after initial qualifications.
SP-R	The service portfolio will provide advance information of service catalog items that will be handled via request management.
R-SC	Request management will own the responsibility to receive the specific transaction-based services published by the service catalog.
SC-R	Service-catalog management will outsource the transaction-based service execution to request management.

Table 9: Interfaces in integration

11.1.5 Process Integration vs. Tool Integration

Tool integration is in fact process integration. Since each process is enabled by one or more tools, the connection of communication and data transfer among those tools is deemed to be tool integration, but the underlying theme is process integration.

The technical part of process integration deals with tools; process integration has a huge dependency on tools. You can implement process integration in a wide variety of ways. Common choices include

1. web services,

2. extract, transform, and load (ETL),

3. communications message protocols,

4. screen scraping,

5. program calls,

6. direct data access, and

7. file transfer.

The advantages of process integration are as follows:

1. Real-time or nearly real-time information access among processes

2. Streamlines ITSM processes and helps raise organizational efficiency

3. Maintains information integrity across multiple processes

4. Ease of operation and maintenance of processes

This requires a fair amount of up-process design, which many organizations are not able to envision or not willing to invest in.

If the tool integration is not driven by the process requirements and undertaken as a pure technical activity, it may not serve the purpose of process integration.

11.2 Multi-Vendor Outsourcing

It is common business scenarios where an IT organization outsources the services to multiple service providers. The most-common scenarios are that the infrastructure is managed by vendor 1, and applications are managed by vendor 2. In this scenario, there are two possibilities—one the process is owned by the IT organization and operated by both the vendors and second the IT organization only has

Single process across multiple vendors

The process operative roles are independent of the organization or position. They agree on common protocol to exchange the task outputs and inputs. They also are governed by a common set of process rules. The process designer ensures efficient protocol and compatible exchange interfaces.

Multi-vendor process operation is the seamless implementation of one single process across multiple service-provider companies as if those companies were the department of the customer company. This kind of implementation unifies the effort of all towers within a company as well as *all* service providers towards *one* single process goal—the process goal written for the customer company and not for the service-provider company.

Multi-vendor process implementations vary in scale and complexity, depending upon the way individual contracts are written, but the key underlying principle is in the area of measurements. The process design demands the complex internal measurement as well as task-level policies, because the tasks will be spread across multiple vendors.

Multiple processes

This scenario requires process integration across multiple vendors. Process engineering for such integration will be based on vendor responsibilities defined in the customer contract. Process split will be based on the split points defined in process. Customer process (prime process) may be a "vantage-point process" with an independent process of vendor, or there can be a master/ slave relationship.

With reference to the integration picture below, we have four integration points:

A—The output of task 1 in prime process becomes the input of vendor 1 process. Vendor 1 operates its own process.

B- The output of vendor 1 process becomes the input for the task 2 of prime process. Vendor 1 ensures that it compatible with prime process. The input/output exchange protocols are the key.

C- The output of task 2 becomes the input for the process of vendor 2.

D- The output of vendor 2's process becomes the input for task 3 of the prime process.

From an end-to-end service perspective, vendors' processes are not visible but deemed to be the task within the prime process.

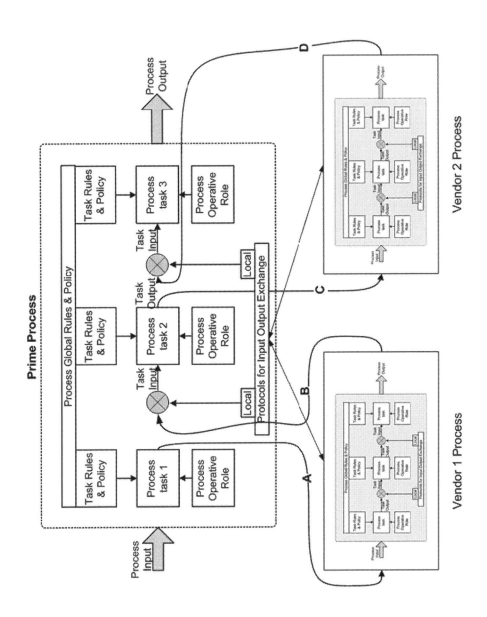

Figure 37: Multivendor process integration

We have seen these concepts working well in industry: how the telecommunication service providers switch data from one carrier to another carrier, how an airline transfers baggage, and how the post office transfers mail. Invariably, multi-vendor processes are required to process a transaction. It works in all businesses, so it would work for IT service as business. All you need is a business-oriented IT to make it work.

12 PROCESS MANAGEMENT AND IT GOVERNANCE

12.1 Governance, Risk Management, and Compliance (GRC)

Governance describes the overall management approach of executive management to direct and control the organization's business by using a combination of management information and hierarchical management control structures. IT governance is a structure of relationships and processes to direct and control the enterprise in order to achieve the enterprise's goals by adding value while balancing risk-versus-return over IT and its processes.

Risk management is the set of processes through which IT governance identifies, analyzes, and mitigates risks that might adversely affect realization of the organization's business objectives. The IT governance also, as a part of risk management, sets the risk appetite that is commensurate with business needs. Risk management, under the IT governance, routinely manages a wide range of risks (e.g., technological risks, commercial/financial risks, information-security risks), external legal and regulatory compliance risks that are considered as the key issues in GRC.

Compliance is one of the required outcomes of IT governance and implies conforming to stated requirements. As one of the responsibilities of governance, compliance is achieved through management processes that identify the applicable requirements (defined, for example in laws, regulations, contracts, strategies and policies), assess the state of compliance, assess the risks and potential costs of noncompliance against the projected expenses to achieve compliance, and hence prioritize, fund, and initiate any corrective actions deemed necessary.

COBIT is an IT governance framework and supporting tool set that allows managers to bridge the gap between control requirements, technical issues, and business risks. COBIT enables clear policy development and good practice for IT control throughout organizations. COBIT emphasizes regulatory compliance, helps organizations to increase the value attained from IT, enables alignment, and simplifies implementation of the COBIT framework.

The basic theme of COBIT is "control" and all IT governance revolves around control. Control (in COBIT) is defined as "the policies, procedures, practices and organizational structures designed to provide reasonable assurance that business objectives will be achieved, and undesired events will be prevented or detected and corrected."

12.1.1 A Complete Process Is More than COBIT Control

The definition of *control* directly maps into the process. In fact, process goes beyond what COBIT controls asks for IT governance.

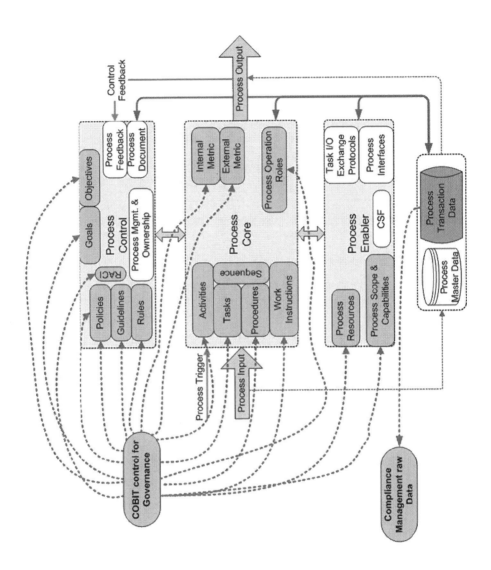

Figure 38: Cobit controls within a process

12.1.2 GRC Tool Myth Busted

Many vendors have jumped into the GRC market with some or other kind of tool to enable GRC. Analysts widely differ on how GRC is defined as market categories. Gartner has stated that the broad GRC market includes the following areas:

1. Finance and audit GRC

2. IT GRC management

3. Enterprise risk management

Tool vendors address the IT GRC management market into the following tool functional segments:

- Controls and policy library

- IT controls self-assessment and measurement

- IT asset repository

- Automated general computer control (GCC) compliance data management

- Remediation and exception management

- Reporting

- Advanced IT risk evaluation and compliance dashboards

- GRC data warehousing and business intelligence

A careful analysis of above functional segments will reveal that the enablement of process life cycle management function is stepping in under the name of GRC. I believe that if you are adequately designing and implementing processes and operating them as designed, you do not need any special tool for GRC. It is like your food habits—if you are taking a healthy and balanced food, you will get *all* your vitamins, proteins, etc. according to your body's needs;

you do not need any artificial dietary supplement, and I intend to elaborate on this.

Controls and policy library

Policy is an integral part of the process. All GRC policies ought to be embedded in the process itself. For example change control policies ought to be part of change management process itself. You do not need any special tool for this. All organizations have collaborative tools such as Share Point or a Wiki-like thing to share the documents. If processes are managed well, the process document will also be maintained and published. An SKMS process, if implemented, will automatically publish the authoritative knowledge about controls and policies around service delivery and support and would be the part of corresponding processes.

IT controls self-assessment and measurement

Yes, assessment and measurement are very important. You need to know where you are before you decide the direction and pace for your destination. But the value of the assessment is in the questionnaire you use for benchmarking and what conclusion you draw from the data you collect through that questionnaire. Therefore, Excel-based tools can serve that purpose as well. Professional tools offer an additional layer of GUI, navigation, data management, historical data comparison, and so on. Basically, the tool collects and stores data in structured form, and that allows you to utilize the data in much more effective manner.

IT asset repository

An asset-management system and CMDB with appropriate control are more a part of the ITSM system rather than the GRC system. In fact, you need asset repository for service-management purposes more than you need it for GRC purposes. GRC needs some additional attributes of an asset to determine if a particular asset is under the GRC scope or not—the attributes that will tell if an asset is important for regulatory compliance or DR compliance.

In other words, if you have implemented a good asset-management system, you have already started collecting the data for GRC purposes.

Automated general computer control (GCC) collection

This is a convenient part of the GRC tool. It provides a common place where you can have the definitions of all controls and use that as a vantage point to link the evidence data and other data for GRC. The data is, of course, generated by other service-management processes. For example, SOX compliance requires that all changes in IT systems are documented and approved before implementing. The GRC tool will list this control and also list the compliance data requirement. From the same place, you can initiate the actions to fetch the data for corresponding control.

Although it is a great convenience, the prerequisite for this is that

a change-management process is implemented with adequate controls; and the process is designed to collect the data for compliance.

Remediation and exception management

This is, in fact, a part of process-management function. If your processes are adequately designed and implemented, remediation and exception handling will happen routinely in operations. You do not need any tool for that.

Reporting

This is also a part of process-management function. If your processes are adequately designed and implemented, there will be a KPI and metric reporting for each process. In fact, that reporting would be beyond GRC and include efficiency and effectiveness KPIs also. The data for reporting is collected by the process execution and reported as a part of service management rather than as GRC requirements.

Compliance reporting will always be a subset of service reporting.

Advanced IT risk evaluation and compliance dashboards

This is again a matter of consolidating data from different sources, providing some commonsense logic, and presenting the data in some fascinating dashboard form. There are many reporting tools that have such capabilities. You can call them a GRC tool if you want to do that.

GRC data warehousing and business intelligence

This is a relatively new offering. GRC vendors are presenting an integrated data framework and are now able to offer custom-built GRC data warehouses and business intelligence solutions. This allows high-value data from any number of existing governance or risk and compliance applications to be collated and analyzed. There is value in it because of the huge convenience of managing the data and compliance reporting.

The aggregation of GRC data using this approach delivers the following benefits:

Existing system and processes can continue without impact.

There is easier transition into an integrated GRC approach, because the initial change is only adding to the reporting layer.

There is real-time ability to compare and contrast data value across systems that previously had no common data scheme.

In a nutshell, GRC tools have the prerequisite that the service-management processes are adequately designed, implemented, and operated as well as sufficiently maintained. And if that is the case, the implementation of a GRC tool primarily is shifting the credit of a good job from regular process management to a GRC function.

12.1.3 Governance by Process-Driven Service Delivery

Governance primarily is a system of right decision-making by the right people. IT governance establishes the fundamental direction for the management framework—a decision-rights and accountability framework for directing, controlling, and executing IT goals in order to determine and achieve desired behaviors and results. IT governance involves defining the management model and creating the (governing) principles. The charter of governance should include

1. who makes what decision in different areas, and what are their authority and responsibilities;

2. how the decisions will be made;

3. how decisions are executed;

4. what information is required to make informed decisions;

5. what decision-making mechanisms should be required;

6. how exceptions will be handled; and

7. how the governance outcome should be reviewed and improved.

Key cornerstones of IT governance are

1. compliance management,

2. financial management,

3. portfolio management, and

4. the governance framework itself.

5. In the next section, we shall see how a process management supports and enables governance.

12.2 Process Enables IT Governance

IT governance is a specific set of interrelated IT processes and practices that need to be viewed and managed from a single vantage point in order to maintain the highest level of governance. It asks for emphasis on performing administration, direction, and controlling activities. Multiple processes are involved in providing effective IT governance. Solutions by themselves do not provide effective governance. Instead, executing effective IT governance practices is the key.

12.2.1 Compliance Management

Although compliance should be considered in the context of all standards, most of the time it is considered in the context of regulatory compliance, and people ignore IT service-quality standard compliance. First of all, the compliance management itself is managed by a compliance management process, so you must have a process to manage the compliance. Secondly, the compliance management process will touch base on other service management processes to operate.

Let us discuss the compliance management process that will typically include the following:

1. Establish compliance-management framework

   a. Define and deploy framework

   b. Define measurements and controls

    c. Define process policies, standards, and conceptual models

    d. Determine process data requirements

    e. Determine process relationships to other processes

    f. Identify process roles and responsibilities

2. Identify compliance requirements

    a. Determine requirements from compliance controls

    b. Maintain compliance requirements catalog

    c. Assess compliance requirements

    d. Create compliance requirements assessment plan

    e. Develop compliance conclusions and recommendations

    f. Identify compliance gaps

    g. Manage a compliance-requirements baseline

3. Define compliance controls ran

    a. Design compliance controls

    b. Specify auditable controls for each compliance requirement

4. Implement compliance controls

    a. Deploy required compliance controls

    b. Verify deployment outcome

5. Audit and report compliance

    a. Certify compliance

    b. Define audit governance

    c. Examine evidence of compliance

    d. Examine records, reports, and logs

    e. Identify gaps and exposures

    f.   Plan audit and request verification

    g.   Verify adherence to procedures

6. Evaluate compliance-management performance

    a.   Assess process execution

    b.   Assess process framework

    c.   Audit process

    d.   Collect evaluation results and collect feedback

    e.   Complete evaluation and produce gap analysis

    f.   Produce process measurements

    g.   Recommend initiatives

What is our take-away from the compliance-management process?

You need to design, implement, and operate the compliance-management process and also need to manage the compliance-management process as defined in this book, and that is what is described in the activities of the process as well.

You need to ensure an adequate level of maturity of other processes that will provide data to the compliance-management process. This again leads to the need to implementing and managing other processes as well.

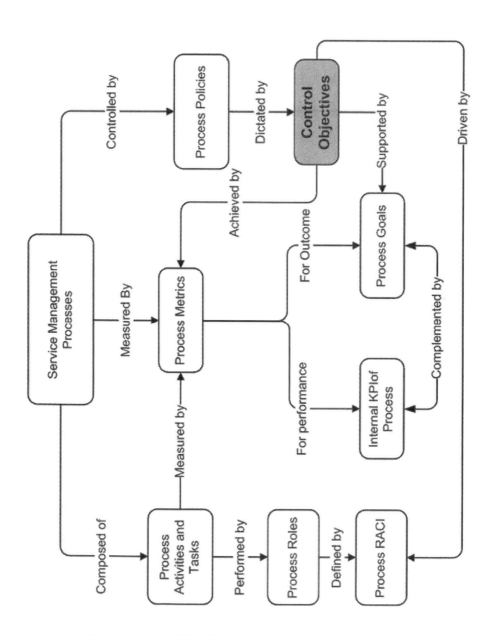

Figure 39: GRC Controls fulfilled by process

Let us take an illustrative case of SOX compliance for change management under general IT controls:

What Control SOX Auditor Examines	How a Process and Process Management Enables It or Provides Evidence of Compliance
Policy—A change-management process is adequately designed and documented and periodically reviewed, which may not allow the introduction of unauthorized or untested modifications into the production environment.	Existence of a process document that is complete and adequately designed. Change-management process is periodically reviewed.
RFC tracking—A change request is initially recorded and analyzed, identifying the scope, potential impact, and quantifying the magnitude of the change request, increasing the risk of significant delays in the implementation of critical system changes and significant cost overruns.	A regular report about the life cycle of all RFCs coming from process establishes that process is being operated as designed.
Testing strategy—A comprehensive test strategy is jointly (by business and IT process owners) defined, reviewed, and implemented, decreasing the likelihood of untested or unauthorized changes introduced into the production environment.	The change-management document establishes levels of testing required for a given level of risk. Business and IT jointly analyze the risk associated with a change as well as define, approve, execute, and document a testing strategy, with the level of testing required based on the assessed risk. Evidence of testing for RFC can be tracked and reported.

What Control SOX Auditor Examines	How a Process and Process Management Enables It or Provides Evidence of Compliance
QA control—Quality-assurance testing procedures ensure that the test versions that are the basis for final reviews and approvals by business/ IT management are in a controlled access environment that prevents modifications subsequent to the review process, decreasing the risk of untested or unauthorized changes being introduced into the production environment.	Quality-assurance testing procedures are performed in a controlled environment that prohibits changes from occurring between testing and moving to production without final approvals from business and IT management. Independent groups (or lock-down procedures) perform change migrations to production (developers cannot make direct, unapproved changes). Evidence of testing comes from the process life-cycle report of every RFC.
Change approvals—Change control procedures to 1. ensure final approvals to implement changes in the production environment; 2. include defined business and IT process owners and impacted business process owners; and 3. confirm that approvals are documented, decreasing the risk of business interruption through the introduction of untested changes.	Evidence of approval is collected and reported from the process operation reports.
Change migration—Control procedures ensure that test versions that are migrated into production are the same as the tested and approved versions of all changes, decreasing the risk of introducing unauthorized or untested changes into the production environment.	Programs and objects test versions that are migrated into production are performed by independent IT groups or via production lock-down procedures. Evidence of compliance comes from the process-operation report.

What Control SOX Auditor Examines	How a Process and Process Management Enables It or Provides Evidence of Compliance
Emergency—An emergency change-management process is 1. adequately defined and documented (including emergency access, post implementation testing and approval procedures); 2. implemented and adhered to; and 3. periodically reviewed, decreasing the risk of the introduction of unauthorized or untested modifications into the production environment.	The change-management policy defines criteria for invoking emergency change-management procedures. Emergency changes require the authorization of an IT director or delegate and are documented and followed according to the change-management process. Emergency change-management procedures are reviewed annually as part of the change-management review process. Evidence of compliance comes from the process-operation report.
Changes to minimum baseline standards—Authorized and reviewed changes occur to the configuration settings, which deviate from the values stated in the minimum baseline standards, resulting in an increased risk of unauthorized access to systems due to consistent, standard baseline configuration settings.	Changes to minimum baseline standards settings, including security role additions or changes, must following the standard change-management process, which includes proper review and authorization by the CCB. Evidence of compliance comes from the process-operation report.
Monitoring changes—Processes to monitor production for unauthorized changes and unauthorized connections to the applications, networks, databases, and Operating Systems are detected. Periodic database and OS monitoring and auditing is performed.	Production applications, databases, and OSs are monitored to detect unauthorized changes and unauthorized connections. Configuration audit reports from the configuration-management process provides the evidence of compliance.

What Control SOX Auditor Examines	How a Process and Process Management Enables It or Provides Evidence of Compliance
Test/development environments— Separate environments exist for test versus production, resulting in only authorized data modification during the testing phase.	Separate environments exist for test versus production. Changes made in the test environment are locked down prior to moving to production. The operation report from process provides the evidence of RFC traversing in multiple environments.

Table 10: SOX compliance enabled by process

12.2.2 Financial Management

The goal of financial management is to assist the internal IT organization with the cost-effective management of the IT resources required for the provision of IT services. A typical set of financial-management activities include the following:

1. Establish financial-management framework

   a. Define process policies, standards, and conceptual models

   b. Deploy framework and assign process responsibilities to organizations

   c. Define measurements and controls

   d. Determine process procedures

   e. Determine process relationships to other processes

   f. Determine process data requirements

2. Perform financial modeling

   a. Perform service valuation

   b. Analyze service investment

   c. Model demand

   d. Review financial modeling results

3. Plan and control budgets

   a. Analyze past and future trends

   b. Apply tracking to the budget entities

   c. Gather the IT budget project list and funding information

   d. Produce the overall budget

   e. Receive budget variance

   f. Revise budget breakdown, if needed

4. Perform financial accounting

   a. Calculate, analyze, and apportion costs

   b. Collect, check, and pay bills to suppliers

   c. Create financial reports

   d. Account for asset depreciation

   e. Gather cost data

   f. Identify and analyze trends

5. Administer charging

   a. Compile and issue bills

   b. Resolve customer discrepancies

   c. Gather charging data and price according to pricing model

   d. Review and update bills

6. Audit financials

   a. Audit financial data

   b. Audit financial procedures

   c. Identify gaps and recommend actions

   d. Review standards and regulations

7. Evaluate financial management performance

   a. Assess process execution

   b. Assess process framework

   c. Collect evaluation results

   d. Produce gap analysis

   e. Recommend initiatives

Now let us examine the key governance questions and how process and process management will address those.

Key Governance Audit Questions	How Financial-Management Process and Process Management Address Governance Audit Questions
Budgeting and planning—What is the process to justify and approve technology-related investment decisions?	Existence of a process and its operation will satisfy this compliance question.
Service costing and charging—How does your group track and manage the cost of IT services?	Cost model is expected to be a part of the financial-management process. Points 2a–2d in the list above will address this.
Has your organization made an effort to recover costs of IT services by operating "IT as a business"?	Points 4 and 5 in the list above will address this. Scope of the process and business alignment of process will satisfy this question.

Key Governance Audit Questions	How Financial-Management Process and Process Management Address Governance Audit Questions
IT accounting—Are total cost of ownership and return on investment figures maintained?	Process operation will provide this data.
Reporting and continuous improvement—What financial-management reports are created, and how frequently are they prepared?	Process operation will provide this data.
What types of checks and balances exist to make sure the financial-management process is working?	Policies and guidelines in the process document will provide the answer.
Quality measurement—How well is the financial-management process performing?	Process management of financial process will provide the answer.
Do you have dedicated financial-management personnel? If so, describe the organization and IT's responsibilities.	Process roles and process ownership will provide this answer.

Table 11: Financial compliance enabled by process

12.2.3 Portfolio Management

The third cornerstone to financial management is portfolio management. The process to govern portfolio management will include the following sub processes:

1. Establish IT portfolio-management framework

2. Inventory IT projects and services

3. Create and maintain IT portfolio categories

4. Assess and prioritize IT portfolio

5. Make IT portfolio decisions and commitments

6. Conduct IT portfolio review

7. Evaluate IT portfolio management performance

If we apply a generic process-management approach, we will not only achieve the goals and the objectives of the portfolio management but also will be able to assure that we will continue to achieve these goals, and that is what governance looks for.

12.3 *Process as Enabler of Transformation*

As I said during the introduction itself that, transformation is a process of profound and radical change that orients the IT organization in a new direction and takes it to an entirely different level of effectiveness. Transformation is not "turnaround," which implies incremental progress on the same plane. Transformation implies a basic change of character that has little or no resemblance with the past configuration or structure. We should also remember that a gradual change over a long period of time can give the illusion of transformation. Therefore, the key characteristics of transformation would be *radical* change and *finite* time. In other words, each transformation will be a project that timeline to deliver outcome, deliverables, and budget.

With this context, let us examine the generally accepted transformation projects. Business transformations are enabled by IT, because business can achieve dramatic results within a short time because of IT enablement. But that is not IT transformation.

Within IT, technology transformation is one of the most common and recognized projects. Large-scale virtualization and migration to cloud is deemed to be technology transformation. Whenever such transformation happens, process redesign would be required, because technology transformation will have direct impact on the service delivery and support. For example, by large-scale virtualization you can dramatically reduce the time to provision a server; you are actually reducing the time for a technical procedure. This procedure is wrapped within a service-management process as given in the diagram in section 2.3.4. To bring in the effect of this on service, you must redesign the process of demand management as well. In a nutshell, process reengineering would be an integral part of any technology transformation project. In fact, most technology transformation projects fail to deliver the full value, because the corresponding service-management processes are not professionally reengineered.

A second case of transformation could be process-transformation projects themselves. Large-scale ITIL projects that were sponsored in many organizations are one such example. In these cases the radical change in the way of working was the outcome that was qualified as transformation. In many cases the change of IT strategy and bringing in new tools are deemed to be transformation. These transformations will surely fail if the purpose of the tool is not met, and of course the purpose lies in process automation.

12.4   Process as an Instrument for Value Addition

Service has always some cost/compensation associated with it. Value is more than or at least equal to the cost/compensation. Value is directly proportional to the benefits and a principle or quality intrinsically desirable. In many cases value defies quantitative measurement. Value is complex, context-specific, and dynamic. Value is like beauty that lies in the eye of the beholder. Value, like service itself, is intangible, and therefore all the principles of service measurement also apply here. Another analogy is customer satisfaction—that is a matter of meeting or exceeding the expectations regardless of service level. Similarly, value is directly related to meeting or exceeding expectations. Also, the actual value vs. perceived value may differ. With all these similarities, we can say the gap model of value is analogous to the gap model of service as explained in section 2.4.1.

SLA for base-lining the value

An SLA is a formal, written, and signed contract between a service provider and a service client. It lists and describes the services to be provided, by whom, with what frequency, and to what standard. It also describes what the service provider is to receive from the client in return. Once compiled and agreed, the SLA forms the sole terms of reference against which the effectiveness or otherwise of the service provider is measured.

An SLA does the following:

1. Defines *what service* will be provided
2. Establishes how the service will be provided
3. Establishes the *quality standard* to be achieved
4. Establishes measurement criteria
5. Establishes reporting criteria
6. Negotiates and determines *cost* of delivery

What we are stating in points 1, 3, and 6 above is benefit and cost. In other words, SLA is the only instrument to establish the value baseline. A service-level management process should also focus on value addition, and that will bring in SLM used for contract arbitration rather than for relationship-building.

Value addition

Value addition (in the form of additional benefits) is provided by an increase in performance potential (of service) without an increase in cost/

compensation. On the other hand, if you reduce the cost to the customer, keeping the same service levels, you are still adding value, but that may not be recognized as value, because the customer is always willing to pay what he or she has written in the contract and yet looks for more service than what is written in the contract. Value addition also includes a reduction in risks associated with conversion of assets into services, but this is more intangible than the service.

So in a nutshell, giving more for the same price is the default value addition. The issue is what is considered as *more*—because you may deliver more, but the customer may still not gain the benefit proportional to that increment. For example, you can buy more memory and more CPU power for the same money as compared to what you were buying in past, but the software and application have also become resource-hungry, and the net effect is same level of benefit. But I would still consider this as value addition, because you have avoided the risk of going obsolete with your resources.

One of the prime examples is from the airline industry. I have observed the standard ticket pricing for last twenty years or so. The price in its absolute term has not increased—in fact, you can consider it decreased if you apply a worldwide inflation factor—however, airlines are decreasing the benefits but keeping the price constant. Now a ticket is just the admission fee, and the rest of the traditional benefits are extra—drinks and food, baggage check, exit-row seat—and yet you'd be right to believe that these are added values.

So in the IT service world, what are these added values? Regarding these, the service provider and customer should be on the same page. Therefore, when you sign SLA, create some value baselines as well. Once **baseline** is understood, the **value addition** will also be visible. *Any* improvement in quality can be regarded as value addition.

ITSM processes are directly contributing to the production of service, hence they would be the prime instrument to add value, and better processes will bring in better value. Following are a few process driven value additions that process improvements have brought in:

Think of a scenario where a service desk is operating an isolated incident management process. In this case, the service desk would be flooded with calls when an e-mail server failed. Users will know of service outages before the service desk knew. After a process transformation project, you have a comprehensive event management process integrated with incident management process, the scenario will change. Now with more effective event management, the service desk knows before users know and thus is more prepared to respond.

User population has increased by over 60 percent, but the ticket count grew by 40 percent, and the service desk staff grew by 20 percent: effective head-count and, consequently, cost reduction.

The number of failed changes has reduced, due to change-management improvements and increased availability of services.

The average time to keep patches in current level was reduced because of better patch-management processes, thus the "vulnerability" period has been reduced.

Increased effectiveness of security management has reduced threats and thus reduced the risk to business.

Of course you shall need numbers, but the good news is that the data will always be collected by the processes, and thus two most-important aspects of value additions are value base-lining and "then–now" comparison.

13 CLOUD SERVICE MANAGEMENT

After our having gone through the process design, implementation, and support in IT service, this section will brief you regarding the applicability of those principles for cloud service management.

13.1 Evolving to a Federated Delivery Model

Over the last three decades, IT has spiraled in complexity and grown from being an enabler of business execution to becoming a key element of differentiation for organizations. This is true in most industries, where IT is now considered a critical part of how businesses can distinguish themselves in the marketplace.

Increasingly, CIOs today are seeking to bring transparency to their assets, standardization to their management, elasticity to accommodating the future, and are looking to leverage the cloud by being more nimble in responding to business. However, IT in most large and distributed enterprise organizations has grown in silos, leading to multiple instances of the same software application, server sprawl, and networking devices.

Today, managing IT is a business in itself, requiring tools and platforms that will allow the CIO and business to

1. Fuse IT with the business;

2. Provide transparency and visibility to business executives;

3. Create a communication platform for IT governance;

4. Enable integrated SLM;

5. Facilitate accountability across disciplines and within service functions; and

6. Enable process, productivity, and efficiency improvement, thus creating an "ERP for IT."

Even as the industry sees maturing growth, CIOs are exploring avenues to deliver IT services management that is aligned to the changes that business is demanding. Some of the current realities and technologies that are driving the need for a changed approach to services management include the following:

Cloud computing and virtualization: Cloud computing technologies offer the benefit of consuming infrastructure/platform/software services as utilities, while virtualization helps to reduce data-center consumption and re-utilization of application logic across the services. These technologies offer enormous potential but are not as simple or transparent to deploy alongside legacy IT ecosystems.

Multi-vendor IT ecosystems: Over the years, businesses have expanded their IT ecosystems to involve specialist vendors in their development and delivery services, thus adding complexity to their IT services management. These expansions have led to duplication of processes and technologies, lack of visibility across vendor landscapes, and increased lag-times to business requirements.

Changing business consumptions of IT services: With the growing trend of blurring personal and corporate spaces and work time zones, business users are expecting to use one computing device to manage their work and private activities. In turn, IT leaders are pushed to deliver services across multiple devices while retaining security of information, device, and application.

13.2 Evolution from Systems Integration to Services Aggregation

With the growing maturity of cloud computing, where the user consumes the hardware-software-connectivity as a service without having to manage any of them, IT services management is now moving from systems integration to services aggregation.

The complexity of putting together infrastructure components and application components is being simplified by prepackaged systems, which have integrated compute/storage/network/virtualization and embedded unified element management. On the applications side, there are a mix of enterprise applications being developed on next-generation agile private or public platforms and SaaS services adoption.

The lines between different approaches (co-location, hosting, data-center outsourcing, infrastructure utility, and cloud computing) are blurring, and these offerings constitute alternate solutions to resolve similar challenges.

The service evolution is happening in the following areas:

Services that are end-user or power-user managed—full self-service

Service that needs a light touch of people but depends upon significant orchestration—orchestrated services

Services that are high-touch and need a consultative and engaged model—high-touch services

13.3   *Synchronizing Multi-Vendor Environments*

Cloud service is inherently a multi-vendor service. With multi-vendor ITIL the strategy should be to bring a platform approach to help IT synchronize their multi-vendor environments without losing business-as-usual availability to their consumers.

Multi-vendor ITIL has seamless implementation of the single and same logical ITIL process across multiple service-provider companies, as if those companies were extensions of the customers' IT department. This unifies the efforts within a company across various service providers toward a single goal, enabling the customer to synchronize all the towers across multiple companies in a service-delivery chain.

Any process should be considered as the asset of the organization that produces the differentiating factor on the end result (outcome).

Tasks within the process produce the deliverable (component for process) and can be outsourced, but the process remains accountable to produce the result.

Multi-vendor ITIL deals with process construction at a micro level, unlike the general implementation of ITIL that deals with process structure at a macro level.

The core discipline of process integration and process engineering detailed in this book is the vantage point to address the multi-vendor implementation complexities of the following:

Maintaining confidentiality of information: Ensure that confidentiality of information is maintained across different companies, even though process might require data-sharing.

Manage conflicts of interests: Vendors have to compete outside the customer's company but collaborate within the customer's company.

Account for geographic distribution: Governing laws and compliance for different nations, complexity, cost of integration, and cost of maintenance.

Ensure process integration: Process integration is one of the key techniques to implement multi-vendor ITIL that connects two or more processes in harmony and in a logical manner, as the tasks within the process are connected in logical manner.

Enable process engineering: Process engineering breaks the core of processes into multiple sets of tasks surrounded by key characteristics: **input, output, rules,** and **roles.**

The outcome of such an approach leads to

1. easy vendor management,

2. facilitating "plug and play" service provider flexibility,

3. switching between service providers more easily (common and consistent process, data definitions),

4. better understanding of the IT services being delivered to the business,

5. a single source of truth for measurement,

6. facilitating standard processes,

7. easy compliance, and

8. continuity of data as vendors change.

13.3.1 Orchestrating IT Services across Environments

This is the beginning of the journey to the cloud. Increasingly, cloud services are a viable and in many cases a critical option for CIOs to consider in parallel to traditional infrastructure and data-center initiatives in IT. These cloud services include system-level capabilities, such as computing, operating systems, storage, or networking, on which the consumer can run a variety of applications being delivered over the cloud.

While they consider services on the cloud, IT needs to guarantee service levels to businesses that they support, while being assured that external service providers are guaranteeing service levels, since it is increasingly rare that services delivered will be completely provided and controlled by the internal IT team.

In essence, IT is increasingly becoming a part of the value chain, and the ability to maximize value for the business and control costs will increasingly rely on extending the management to key control points across the value chain.

Hence, IT of tomorrow requires the organization to become expert in services orchestration and aggregation, enabling a very elastic and dynamic infrastructure/application fabric for business consumption.

Having worked with various customers over the years in enabling them to take a rational approach to cloud adoption, we believe there are four key drivers in deciding whether to consume services on the cloud:

- Turnaround time for the services
- Elasticity in availability
- Ownership and control
- Financial-management drivers

Depending on the requirements of each of these drivers, one has created the right service-delivery platform for a cloud adoption. For example, although businesses may consume Salesforce.com as a service, IT organizations are still held responsible for security, governance, and compliance.

Our view is that ITIL has taken two different kinds of approaches for IT service management. The first approach is a "service factory approach," which is a prominent theme of ITIL v2. In this approach, data centers are viewed as IT service factories, where variety of machines and gears are used to produce an IT service. This service then is delivered to a consumer station via network pipes. The second approach, which is a prominent theme for ITIL v3, is the "service life cycle approach," which talks about the states or phases in a cyclic manner and maintains focus on the process to manage the state.

In order to implement cloud service management, we has combined these two approaches and added a pragmatic implementation focus with significant emphasis on agility, simplicity, and service integration in managing the entire cloud service chain.

We believes that the cloud service delivery chain will include the roles of a service creator, service aggregator, service deliverer, service consumer, and a service bill-payer. These roles may exist all within one entity or can span across multiple entities.

The below illustration gives a simplified view of the value chain:

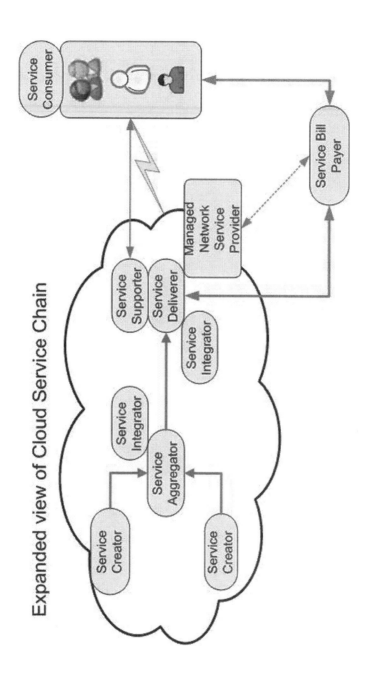

Figure 40: Cloud service chain

The following are the key aspects one needs to consider during process integration and engineering for cloud service management and look for capabilities in platforms that can cover the life cycle:

- Self Service for better User Experience

  o Service catalog

  o Request management

  o Dashboards and Reporting

- Orchestration to automate activity

  o Policy automation

  o Dynamic infrastructure services provision

  o Dynamic application landscape deployment

  o User Provisioning across Applications

  o Resource Lifecycle Management

- Metering

  o Service consumption

  o Service Asset management

  o Service accounting, chargeback & billing

- Monitor

  o Performance/availability/Usage monitoring

  o Event Management, Analytics and probable cause

  o Configuration and Security Event Monitoring

Features related to managing the service life cycle of the cloud include the following:

- Governance
    - Demand & Service Portfolio Management
    - Compliance and risk management
    - Business Continuity and Disaster Recovery
    - Agile Services and Applications Development
- Assurance and Service Levels
    - Service Level Management
    - Contract Management
    - Supplier Management
- Security
    - Identity Federation across Services
    - Identity Governance and Access Control management
    - Data Loss Prevention Techniques
- Service Operations
    - Change and Release Management
    - Configuration Management and CMS
    - Incident and Problem Management

In summary, the crux of evolving into a hybrid delivery fodel is to have a very strong service-management-centric approach to running IT. Also, consider the fact that that most service-management approaches tend to focus on just process, technology, and people. There are two most-important aspects that drive the people to use the process enabled by technology. That is about having a strong vision and steering that vision into implementation, which happens with a strong cultural effect of how one focuses on people, who are the central theme to enable this to work. In this book we have cited many examples of where people's empowerment and enablement is the key to success.

Annexure

This annexure describes the process developed with the illustration in section 6

ANNEXURE A

1   IMPORTANCE OF PATCH MANAGEMENT

Before the widespread adoption of Microsoft server operation systems at enterprise level, patch management was an "install and forget" practice; once deployed, many systems were infrequently or never updated. The rise of widespread worms and maliciously code-targeting known vulnerabilities on unpatched systems, especially Microsoft operating systems, and the resultant downtime and expense they bring has forced all organizations to focus on patch management. Along with these threats, increasing concern around governance and regulatory compliance (e.g., HIPAA, Sarbanes-Oxley) has also forced enterprises to gain better control and oversight of their systems. Also, pervasive interconnections with the outside world made it mandatory to secure your system with the latest patches. So patch management has become a critical issue.

While the issue of patch management has technology at its core, it's clear that focusing only on technology to solve the problem is not the answer. Installing patch-management software or vulnerability-assessment tools without supporting guidelines, requirements, and oversight will be a wasted effort that will further complicate the situation. Instead, solid patch-management programs will team technological solutions with policy and operationally based components that work together to address each organization's unique needs. And this is what we are addressing through this patch-management process.

1.1   Goals and Objectives

The goal of the patch-management process is to create a consistently configured environment that is secure against known vulnerabilities in the operating system and consequently in application software.

Objectives of patch management include

1.   enabling audit-friendly procedure for compliances and collecting compliance evidence data,

2.   minimizing service interruption,

3.   monitoring and measuring the effectiveness of patch deployment, and

4.   making the operation deterministic and without surprises.

1.2   Scope

1.2.1 Server Scope

Server scope includes all Windows servers that are running approved server images.

1.2.2 Patches in scope

- Security update—a released fix for OS security-related vulnerability. Security vulnerabilities will be rated based on their severity. The severity rating is indicated in the Microsoft security bulletin as critical, important, moderate, or low.

- Critical update—a broadly released fix for a specific problem that addresses a critical, non-security-related bug.

- Update—a broadly released fix for a specific problem. An update addresses a non-critical, non-security-related bug.

1.2.3 Scope exclusion

1. Integrated service pack—the combination of a product and a service pack in one package

2. Feature pack—new product functionality that is first distributed outside the context of a product release and that is typically included in the next full product release

3. Upgrade—software package that replaces an installed version of OS with a newer version

4. Hotfix—single, cumulative package that includes one or more files that are used to address a problem in OS.

5. Service pack—a tested, cumulative set of all hotfixes, security updates, critical updates, and updates

Note: These exclusions will be managed by a regular change-management process.

1.3 Policies

1. A patch for fixing vulnerability will be considered as emergency or critical and will be deployed in an expedited mode; all other patches will be normal (non-critical).

2. If multiple patches need to be applied, then we shall bundle them. If any one patch in this bundle is emergency, then the entire bundle will be treated as an emergency.

3. All the patches will be applied in the testing and development servers first, before deploying to any environment. Some legacy applications don't have a testing or development environment, and owners of those applications would have right to decline the patch.

4. The patch-testing on these servers will be OS-level testing only. This includes sanity checks that the server is running after reboot, all services are running, all file system and disks are mounted properly, and CPU/memory is not clogged, etc. The application team will be responsible to test the application functionality and post patching activities, and this will be part of the RFC.

5. Patch will be deployed through <Tools> or manually in development, testing, and production environments.

6. Patch deployments in development, testing, and production environments will be under change control and will be governed by change-management processes.

7. An approved RFC for a patch or a bundle of patches will imply that the risk and downtime associated with that patch are acceptable as described in RFC.

8. While submitting an RFC for patch deployment in production, the submitter must link it to the RFC for that patch in a development and testing environment. The change manager will verify that the development and testing RFC was successfully resolved before initiating the approval process for production deployment. He will not accept the RFC for production deployment if it is not linked to the developmental and testing RFC, *and* that RFC was not successful.

9. Antivirus signature releases will be auto-deployed and downloaded from the site itself and don't fall under server patch management.

10. Legacy systems, which are intentionally kept outdated with the latest patch, will be an exception to this process and will be tracked separately.

11. An OS patching window should not coincide with application patching or an application-maintenance window.

12. CMDB should contain details about each managed server in the environment. CMDB will be deemed to be an authorized data source.

1.4 Input/output

Following are the key inputs and outputs for the input/output process:

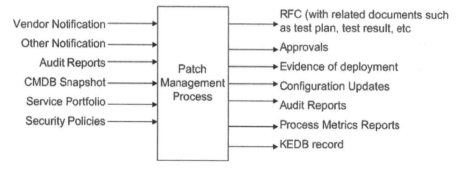

1.5 Process Prerequisites

This process relies upon the

1. existence of adequately mature configuration management database,

2. existence of change-management process,

3. existence of security policies, and

4. server image management process (if server image is deemed to be CI, then prerequisite 1 will cover this).

2 PROCESS OVERVIEW

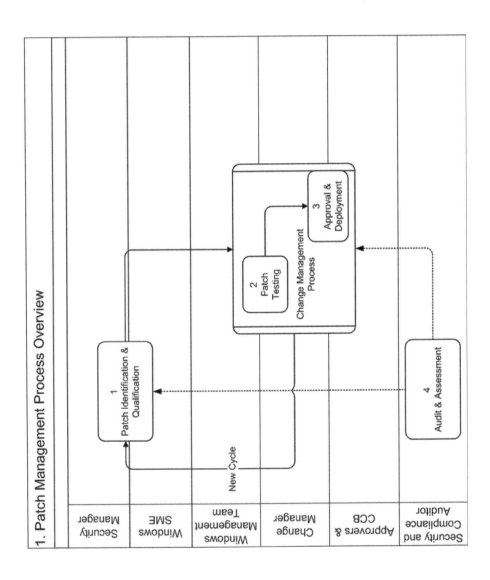

2.1 Process Cycle

A patch cycle establishes scheduling guidelines and plans for a comprehensive patch-management program. A patch cycle guides the normal application of patches and updates to systems in scope.

A patch cycle has three sub processes that are repeated every month at a pre-defined day of the month. The fourth sub process—audit and assessment—is external to the process cycle but is part of the process for certain operational tasks that are triggered by this sub process.

Step	1	2	3	4	5	6	7	8
Non critical patch	Second Tuesday of month	Second Wednesday of Month	Second Friday of Month	Second Friday of Month	Third Wednesday of Month	Third Wednesday of Month	Third Friday of Month	Third Saturday of Month
Emergency Patch	Second Tuesday of month	Second Wednesday of Month	Second Thursday of Month	Second Thursday of Month	Second Friday of Month	Second Friday of Month	Second Saturday of Month	Second Sunday of Month

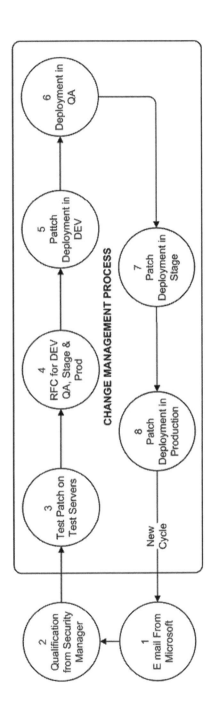

CHANGE MANAGEMENT PROCESS

2.1.1 Patch Calendar Agreement

Change management will publish the patch-management calendar on a quarterly basis. The calendar will be published and distributed to the data-center contact distribution list. Any change in the patch calendar will be under change control.

The calendar will specify the specific groups and sub groups of the systems that will be patched on specific days in the cycle. In automatic deployment by tool, the calendar is the key input for tool configuration.

Application teams may submit an RFC with their requested quarterly calendar if the application is on a dedicated server. The RFC will follow the normal change-control process. This request for a new patch calendar must be submitted at least three weeks before the beginning of the quarter.

3 ACTIVITY DETAILS

3.1 *Identify Patch*

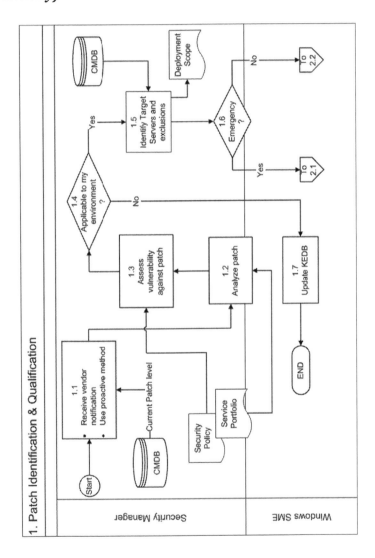

3.2

3.2.1 Patch Identification

Either the security manager or SME will receive the notification of the patch release. This notification usually provides the product versions and details of what the patch does. Notification does not include the patch but includes the information about the patch. There may be multiple patches' information in one notification. The security manager will use the information in notification to identify the correct patch that needs to be analyzed. Vendor notification may not be the only source of information. Organizations may adopt proactive methods, such as subscription to organizations such as patchmanagement.org.

3.2.2 Patch Analysis and Assessment

The patch analysis is jointly done by the security manager and SME. This will focus on a very specific aspect of the patch in the context of the organization's environment. For example, some patches may be applicable to the compatibility of Windows with third-party databases, and the organization may not have those databases. Analysis will also focus on the vulnerability that is being targeted and the extent of threat. It will address the question of how the patch will contribute to mitigation of those risks.

3.2.3 Patch Qualification

Patch qualification includes a formal decision about moving forward with patch deployment. There may be variety of factors, including the security policies to make such a decision. Security manger decision will be final and binding. They will be supported by an adequate level of analysis conducted with the help of SME.

For non-security patches, SME will analyze with the collaboration of other process managers—primarily the availability manager and the capacity manager.

3.2.4 Deployment Scoping

Deployment scoping includes the geography domain, sub domain, and sub nets in scope, and it will include which server will be targeted and which server will be excluded. It will also establish the exact schedule within the cycle time.

3.3 Test Patch

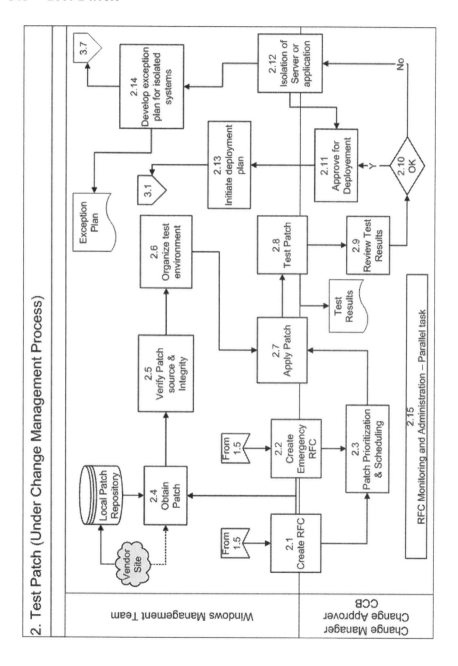

3.3.1 Patch Downloading

Patch will always be downloaded from the vendor's site only. Depending upon the level of automation, tools can be configured to automatically download, but in any case a patch repository will be maintained within the organization. This patch repository will be maintained as an extension of DSL (definitive software library). All other deployment will pick up the patch from this location.

3.3.2 Patch Verification

This step helps ensure that the update is valid and has not been maliciously or accidentally altered. Digital signatures or some form of check-sum or integrity verification will be a component of patch validation. This signature will be regularly verified, especially as an update is passed through an organization's server team (on the update server, in build images, an in software repositories).

3.3.3 Organizing Test Environment

Attempts will be made to obtain the test environment that mirrors production as closely as possible, for at least the majority of critical applications and supported operating platforms. Testing environment could be a subset of production systems, such as an ad hoc test environment or department-level servers.

3.3.4 RFC for Change Management

For every patch there will be one RFC in the change-management system. RFC will always be submitted by a Windows management team as soon as the patch has been qualified by the security manager. All the activities from this point onward will be under the supervision of change-management process, and all the policies of change control will apply.

3.3.5 Patch Testing

Patch testing would be a mandatory requirement regardless of criticality. The patch-testing rigor will relate directly to the criticality of systems and data handled and the complexity of the environment.

Once a patch has been determined valid, it will be placed in a test environment. Testing will be done only in authorized test environments. In order to minimize the testing risks and testing irrelevance, the following guidelines will be applicable:

- Unknown operating environment—only approved server images will be considered in scope.

- Adequate and dedicated testing resources will be planned and provisioned.

- Time constraints and delay will be avoided by adherence to the pre-defined schedule.

- Blind patch deployment will be prevented through enforcement of change-control policy.

The patch-testing focus will be narrowed after reviewing which applications are present on the servers targeted by new patches. After reviewing the configuration information of the entire CMDB, a decision will be made to find ways to exclude as many of those assets as possible from actual patch testing. Once the patch is installed, run the impacted applications to see if the patch has negatively affected their performance and behavior.

3.3.6 Test Results and Consequential Plan

If all the applications function properly, the patch is safe to deploy. If any of the applications malfunction or crash, the patch is incompatible.

If a tester discovers that a security patch is negatively impacting the performance of one or more applications, he or she will notify the SME, who will explore another option—isolating the impacted application—before deciding whether to deploy the patch to those servers running the impacted software. During this time the application owners will be involved with Windows SMEs to facilitate the isolation of an application so that it always loads the versions of components—such as DLLs—with which it was originally developed and tested. This could be accomplished by providing DLLs and other shared components for the impacted application and placing information traditionally stored in the registry into manifests that specify the location of these components. By successfully isolating the application, the incompatible patch would be cleared to alter the OS files without affecting the isolated software.

If the detected impact cannot be resolved through isolation, the SME will carefully evaluate the business value of the impacted application versus the significance of the vulnerability corrected by the security patch. In some cases the SME would collaborate with the security manager to implement additional layers of security to limit the vulnerability and exploitability of the critical, unpatched environment. Some options include additional access controls through firewalls.

3.3.7 Initiate Deployment

The initial phases of production rollout will be considered an additional component of the testing process. Rollouts will be done in tiers in accordance with the patch calendar, with the initial tiers involving less-critical systems. Based on the performance of these stages of the patch-deployment process, the entire environment will be updated, and the testing process will be considered finished with the completion of final acceptance testing.

3.4   *Deploy Patch*

Installation and deployment are where the actual work of applying patches and updates to production systems occurs. And while this stage is the most visible to the organization as a whole, the effort expended throughout the entire patch-management process is what dictates the overall success of a given deployment and the patch-management program in total.

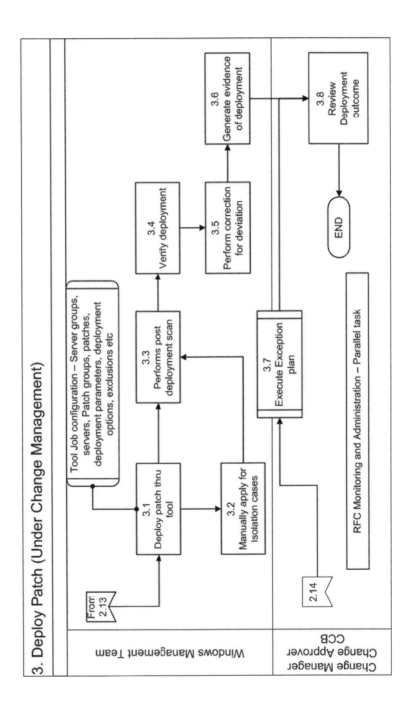

3. Deploy Patch (Under Change Management)

Windows Management Team

Change Manager
Change Approver
CCB

From 2.13

3.1 Deploy patch thru tool

Tool Job configuration – Server groups, servers, Patch groups, patches, deployment parameters, deployment options, exclusions etc

3.2 Manually apply for isolation cases

3.3 Performs post deployment scan

3.4 Verify deployment

3.5 Perform correction for deviation

3.6 Generate evidence of deployment

3.7 Execute Exception plan

2.14

3.8 Review Deployment outcome

END

RFC Monitoring and Administration – Parallel task

3.4.1 Deployment Plan

A deployment plan will be based on two factors that may vary slightly in each cycle, namely Patch-based deployment and System-based deployment

Reboot policy

Deployment of certain patches that are related to OS components may force an immediate reboot—a critical operation for many environments, especially when production servers are involved. Process will adopt a flexible reboot policy that allows administrators to customize reboots after patch deployment.

Pilot deployment and full-scale deployment

The security manager and change manager may decide to pilot certain deployments before full-scale deployment. This will be based on the assessment of the impact.

3.4.2 Deployment through Tools

Automated patch deployment will be applicable only for the "push" part of deployment. In other words, no patch will be automatically downloaded and deployed. Every patch must go through the change controls.

Additional technical controls will be applied to restrict when and by whom tool configuration and actions will be triggered.

3.4.3 Manual Deployment

All the systems that are excluded from tool deployment will be patched manually. It is expected that there will be only a handful of such systems. Adequate resource provisioning will ensure timely manual deployment.

3.4.4 Post-Deployment Scan

A post-deployment scan will be run after the deployment cycle. For manually deployed systems, a separate report will be produced and appended with the scan report.

3.4.5 Verification and Corrective Actions

A compliance report will serve two purposes:

1. Provide the evidence of patch deployment

2. If deployment of some system failed, it will provide the list of systems that require manual correction.

3.4.6 Evidence of Deployment

A system-generated scan report as well as a log file report will be acceptable evidence of deployment. Evidence will be submitted before the closure of RFC.

3.5 Audit and Assess

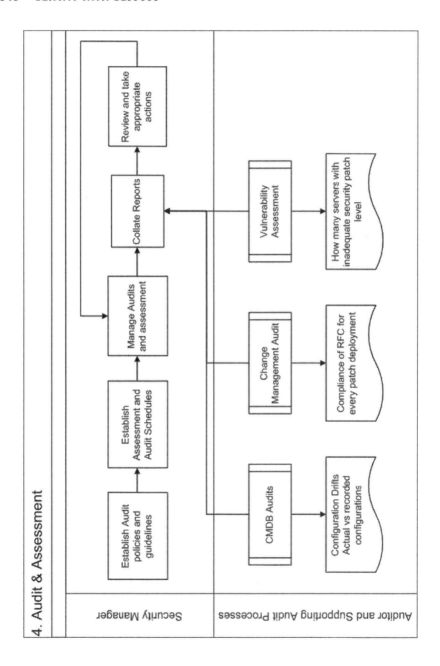

3.5.1 Audit Policies and Guidelines

Audit policies and guidelines will be dictated by corresponding processes, such as security management, configuration management, and change management.

3.5.2 CMDB Audit

The configuration-management process will have its own audit to facilitate the accuracy and currency of CMDB that serves the patch management process's making appropriate decisions. The patch-management scan report will also serve this audit by providing the information about configuration drifts (actual vs. recorded configurations).

3.5.3 Change-Management Audit

Proper control of RFC for every patch deployment will be one of the primary compliance requirements. Change-control process as a whole will be within the compliance scope for general IT control compliance.

3.5.4 Vulnerability Assessment

Vulnerability assessment will provide a clear picture on

- what systems need to be patched for any given vulnerability or bug, and
- if the systems that are supposed to be updated are actually patched.

The vulnerable-systems report gives away the details of the healthy and vulnerable systems. This patch report is essentially important to reduce the risks that are associated with the presence of vulnerable systems.

The vulnerable-patches report will list the missing patches. The report will also provide the details of the affected systems in the environment for every patch that is listed.

The supported-patches report will provide the details of all the patches released by Microsoft Corporation, irrespective of whether these patches have a relation to our environment. The supported-patches report will be useful for future plans to upgrade the systems as well as the server-image-management process.

3.5.5 Compliance

A combination of all three audits and assessments will form the compliance report. The compliance report requirements will be set by internal as well as external auditors.

3.6 Roles and Responsibilities

3.6.1 Security Manager

All the responsibilities of the security manager in the process of patch management will be dictated and inherited from the security-management process. In the context of patch management, key responsibilities include but are not limited to

1. identifying patches and qualifying patches,

2. establishing audit policies and guidelines,

3. establishing assessment and audit schedules,

4. managing audits and assessment, and

5. reviewing audit reports and taking appropriate actions.

3.6.2 Windows SME

Key responsibilities of the Windows SME include but are not limited to

1. working with the security manager to qualify the patch,

2. helping change-management to perform risk assessment,

3. resolving technical problems,

4. reviewing test results, and

5. developing exception plans for isolated systems.

3.6.3 Windows Management Team

The role of implementer in the change-management process includes but is not limited to

1. applying patches,

2. testing patches, and

3. executing exception plans for isolated systems.

3.6.4 Change Management

Change management oversees the entire end-to-end process and ensures all the process resources are available as well as that all the process strength is extended to patch management.

3.6.5 Auditor

An audit is a tool for risk management and not a tool for policing or punishing. Key responsibilities of an auditor include (as applicable to CMDB data accuracy and currency, change-management process-control effectiveness and the vulnerability of Windows servers) the following:

1. Assessing the current state:

    — Provide advice and assist with current-state assessments, and gap

    — If required, independently verify assessment results

    — Provide independent assurance that issues identified are valid, business cases are subjectively and accurately presented, and plans appear achievable

    — Provide expert advice and guidance where appropriate.

2. Monitoring control initiatives:

    — Provide independent assessment of the overall efficiency and effectiveness of respective system or process

    — Provide feedback on and consider the effectiveness of audit's contribution to the initiative

    — Use positive results to improve current audit-related activities

    — Use lessons learned to adapt and improve audit's approach to future IT audit activities

3.7   *Measurements and Reporting*

Change-management measurement and reporting will apply. In addition to that, the following metrics will be applicable to measure the effectiveness of process:

1. Percentage patch coverage per IP subnet—(patch found*100)/(Patch Found + Missing Patch)

2. Percentage critical patch coverage per IP subnet (Critical patch found*100)/(Patch Found + Missing Critical Patch)

3. Percentage patches deployed by tool

4. Configuration drifts discovered

5. Patches deployed within patch cycle

3.8 Interfaces with Other Processes

The patch-management process is in fact a version of change-management process; therefore, all the interfaces of change management process apply here:

1. There may be a security incident that may lead to an emergency fix.

2. Proactive problem management may discover some security hole that may lead to patch deployment.

3. Patch management must maintain the availability and performance SLA's established by the SLM process.

ABOUT AUTHORS

Prafull Verma

Prafull Verma has a bachelor's degree in electronics and communication Engineering and has over thirty years' experience in the area of electronic data processing and information technology. He started his career in India in the area of electronic data processing systems and later moved to the US in 1997. During the past thirty years, he has worked on diversified areas in computer science and information technologies. Some of his key experience areas are the design and implementation of heterogeneous networks (LAN and WAN), midrange technical support management, end user service management and design, and the implementation and management of process-driven ITSM systems.

Prafull has acquired a unique blend of expertise in integrated areas of tools, process, governance, operations, and technology. He is the author of several methodology and frameworks for IT service management that includes multi-vendor ITIL frameworks and ITSM for cloud.

Prafull's competencies and specializations include the area of merging engineering with service management, as this book manifests, and outsourcing business management.

Currently, Prafull is working for HCL Technologies Ltd, Infrastructure Service Division, -Cross Functional Service Business Unit, as Global Practice Director and Principal Architect

Kalyan Kumar

Kalyan Kumar (KK) is the Chief Technology Architect for HCL Technologies – ISD and leads all the Global Technology Practices in the Infrastructure Services Division. In his current role Kalyan is responsible defining Architecture & Technology Strategy, New Solutions Development & Engineering across all ISD Practices including Enterprise Infrastructure, Business Productivity, Unified Communication Collaboration & Enterprise Platform/DevOps Service Lines. Kalyan is also responsible for Business and

Service Delivery for Cross Functional Services & Leveraged Cloud Services in HCL ISD.

Kalyan is widely acknowledged as an expert and path-breaker on BSM/ITSM & IT Architecture and Cloud Platforms and has developed many IPs for the company in these domains. He is also credited with building HCL ISD's MTaaSTM Service from the scratch, which has a multi-million turnover today and a proprietary benchmark for Global IT Infrastructure Services Delivery. His team is also credited with developing the MyCloudSM platform for Cloud Service Management & MyDevOps which is a pioneering breakthrough in the Utility Computing and Hybrid Agile Ops Model space. He has been presented with many internal and industry awards for his thought leadership in the IT Infrastructure Management space.

Kalyan also runs the HCL ISD IPDEV Incubator Group where he is responsible for incubating new services, platforms and IPs for the company. Kalyan has spoken at many prestigious industry platforms and is currently actively engaged in Partner Advisory Board of BMC Software, CA Technologies etc.

In his free time Kalyan likes to jam with his band Contraband as a drummer /percussionist.

You can follow Kalyan Kumar on Twitter @KKLIVE and at Linkedin (http://www.linkedin.com/in/kalyankumar.)

28606306R00187

Made in the USA
Charleston, SC
17 April 2014